MEAT *on* THE SIDE

MEAT *on* THE SIDE

Delicious Vegetable-Focused
Recipes for Every Day

NIKKI DINKI

Photographs by
ELLEN SILVERMAN

St. Martin's Griffin
New York

For more pics of the recipes, reviews, video recipes, tips, and more, check out NikkiDinkiCooking.com.

Prop stylist: Bette Blau
Food stylist: Roscoe Betsill
Book design: Shubhani Sarkar

www.stmartins.com

The Library of Congress Cataloging-in-Publication Data is available upon request.

ISBN 978-1-250-06716-6 (paper over board)

ISBN 978-1-4668-7519-7 (e-book)

Our books may be purchased in bulk for promotional, educational, or business use. Please contact your local bookseller or the Macmillan Corporate and Premium Sales Department at 1-800-221-7945, extension 5442, or by e-mail at MacmillanSpecialMarkets @macmillan.com.

First Edition: June 2016

10 9 8 7 6 5 4 3 2 1

For
EVAN
and my
WILLA

Contents

Salads

Sandwiches, Tacos + The Like

Tacos

Pizzas + Flatbreads

Pasta + "Pasta"

Light Meals

Soups

Main Meals

Introduction

I'M NINE YEARS OLD, IT'S DINNERTIME ONCE
again, and I'm sitting at the table surrounded by
my family, including my sisters and my newborn
brother. When you come from a big family (especially a family of Dinkis) it can be hard at times
to get noticed, and as a born performer I was
always looking for an audience. But not on this
particular night. Tonight I let everyone else
upstage me and even keep calm when my older
sister makes "that face," which would normally
get a rise out of me. Tonight is different. Tonight
I have a plan.

Being the creative person that I am, I had
concocted a new way I could get out of eating the
wholesome food my mother had a habit of putting
in front of me night after night. I had exhausted
my usual go-to techniques: I needed a new plan
and I had a genius idea; tonight the injustice would
end. Tonight I had the best plan yet. Tonight
"Picky Nikki" (I hated that name) was taking it to
a whole new level.

The mission started at 5:03 P.M. I waited until
the regular dinnertime commotion commenced
and I made my move. Casually, but not too casually, I got up from the table with my little heart
racing, palms sweating, and most important, plate
in hand. As I reached the family room, I found
what I had predetermined was to be the landfill
for my mother's meal: an open heating vent. After
I pushed the last of my broccoli into the dark un-
known, I quietly returned to the table and declared
myself finished—a member of the clean-plate club.

To my mother's immense satisfaction, she released
me from the table and I ran away, grabbing a quick
string cheese on my way out.

I was a genius—it was the perfect plan. Except
that I had not accounted for the smell wafting up
from the vent the next week. After a long investiga-
tion by my father to discover where the awful scent
was coming from, I finally came clean. Once my
parents were done contemplating how a nine-year-
old snuck away from the table with her plate in
tow without anyone noticing, it was obvious that
new rules were needed. I expected the worst, but
somehow got the best. To my complete satisfaction,
my mother declared that I could eat whatever I
wanted. However, she would not be a short-order
cook, and I would have to make do by myself. My
reaction? AMAZING! I was free! I went to work as
a mini restaurateur, creating nutritious dishes for
my menu including, and pretty much limited to,
cereal, toasted bagels, slices of American cheese,
and ramen noodle soup. What about vegetables
you ask? Ha, never! Protein? Doesn't American
cheese count? Anyway, who needed such things?! I
was completely content with my bread, cheese, and
cereal diet.

Before I knew it, I was twenty years old and
trying to convince myself that these things composed a proper diet. It was hard to explain to my
new friends in New York City that I could eat only
the white rice if we went to a sushi restaurant, or
only the bread basket anywhere else. Most of the
time, I simply didn't make dinner plans because

that I was actually developing a taste for these new foods. The first time I had a tomato I hated it. The second, third, and fourth times were not much better. But by the tenth time, it was tolerable and somewhere around my twentieth time tasting a tomato, I actually liked it. My brain started racing. What about all the other things I hadn't tried yet? I had started with vegetables, and then after years of eating a vegetarian diet I slowly added fish, then chicken, and finally pork and red meat to my diet. My relationship with food completely changed. Food became a fun, enjoyable adventure and I couldn't wait to experiment with my newfound palate by cooking at home.

When I started cooking, I felt like a novice, but a natural, too. I started sautéing onions and using my oven, and the key to my success was that I messed up enough times to learn exactly how to do it right and make it foolproof. I watched every cooking show, read every book on the subject, took over one hundred hours of classes, and kept on cooking and cooking. It became an extreme hobby. Before I knew it, cooking had taken over my life in the most fantastic of ways.

I had spent my noncooking years pursuing acting, photography, and writing, so it seemed natural to me to combine them all. My husband came home from work one day and I announced I was going to put cooking videos online and start a blog, and that I would be working toward a goal of one day having my own cooking show. I knew that I could make people excited about a whole new way of cooking. I had taken a unique journey with food, and developed a unique cooking perspective because of it. Since vegetables were my gateway into the culinary community, I always thought of them first, and I never stopped learning about and experimenting with them. I cooked meat, too, but I cooked the meat on the side, making vegetables the star of the dish and never using more than 4 ounces

it was always awkward, and there were never any good answers to their questions as to why I ate this way. I was well aware that I couldn't go on like this forever. I had learned long ago that cheese, bread, and cereal do not make up the essential food groups. I had probably stunted my growth and I felt gross all the time, but most of all I was embarrassed by my eating habits. I knew things had to change and was determined to change them.

I made it my mission to start trying new things. At first, I just resisted the urge to convulse as vegetables hit my lips. I made sure to eat in low light so the food looked slightly less scary; oh, and wine helped, too. My initial goal was to simply get to a point where I could swallow regular food that might be served at a restaurant and not look like I was in pain as I ate it. This seemed like it would make me a more popular dinner companion.

Then something amazing happened. I noticed

of meat per portion. Now, it was time to share this perspective and my excitement with the world!

I went right to work. My first cooking videos were extremely popular and my new fans wanted more. Soon after my first few posts, I met a radio producer who wanted to put me and my food ideas on the air, soon allowing me to wield the mic every week on WBAI 99.5 FM in New York City. Of course, if I was on the radio, I needed a Web site that would serve as a hub for my ideas, recipes, and demonstrations. So I launched a Web site called NikkiDinkiCooking.com. I sat down and looked around at this new life I had created and realized that when something feels right, it just works.

One phone call changed it all: They wanted me to be a contestant on Season 9 of *Food Network Star*, the Food Network's most prestigious and highest rated show, where 12 contestants compete to have their own show. There was nothing to say,

I only smiled and shook my head in disbelief. Two weeks later, I left my home and all that was normal. For more than two months I lived a different life on a different coast. My time spent in LA was stressful, insane, nerve-racking, and challenging but also one of the most fantastic experiences of my life.

The first assignment we were given was to tell Bobby Flay, Giada DeLaurentiis, and Alton Brown exactly who we were and the unique perspective we were going to bring to the show. When it was my turn I told the Food Network judges about me and about what defines me as a cook.

I told them that "meat on the side" was the phrase that defined the way I cooked and ate. They heard about my food revolution and how vegetables had been my first love and were always the star of my plates. They all smiled when I explained that to create a dish I always start by thinking

about how I want the vegetables to shine: How I will prepare them, what I want them to taste like, and what textures I want there to be. Finally, I told them that after I have created a balanced and composed dish, I then think about what protein I want to include in the meal. By focusing on the veggies first, I create complete meals—with or without the meat. They loved it.

As my journey came to an end on *Food Network Star* (I was this close), I knew I would find another path. The word about meat on the side spread; doors started opening and I finally got my own show on the Cooking Channel. Every week on *Junk Food Flip* I stand next to Bobby Deen and share my food on a grand scale and literally nothing makes me happier. And now, after blood,

sweat, and tears (and I do not exaggerate), I also get to share 100+ recipes with you in this book.

The *Meat on the Side* cookbook needed to be written because there is a huge group of people who are already eating this way. There are people who are looking to save money and buy less high-priced proteins while providing their family with a more well-rounded meal. There are also people who are trying to cut back on the amount of meat they eat in one sitting, in line with the USDA recommendations that we eat only 5 to 6 ounces of meat per day. Lastly, *Meat on the Side* provides new and exciting ways to prepare veggies, making every meal more nutritious, with fewer calories than the meat-heavy alternatives. *Meat on the Side* places vegetables in their rightful place: as star of the dish.

How to Use This Book—What to Look For

WE ARE ALL UNIQUE PEOPLE WITH UNIQUE situations, stories, and tastes. Some of us have kids, and some of us have picky husbands who may as well be our kids. Some of us can eat whatever we want, and never gain an extra pound, but most of us can't. And some of us spend weekends relaxing and simmering sauces for hours while others have workweeks that blur well into our weekends. So, if you're looking to cook and eat in ways that fit your lifestyle, I've made that easy for you: Just use the following keys to quickly find recipes that are easily switched from meatless to meaty, family approved, calorie controlled, or perfect for when you need dinner on the table ten minutes ago.

Make It Meaty— It Doesn't Have to Be Vegetarian

I find that as long as something is tasty I don't really care if there is meat in the dish or not. So when creating recipes for this book I was fine with including ones that were completely vegetarian as long as they were also simply scrumptious. But just because some of my recipes are meat-free doesn't mean there are not super tasty options for easily adding meat to them. So when you need a little extra protein punch, or are looking to make a light vegetarian meal a bit more substantial, look for "Make It Meaty" to find my suggestions for easy ways to add a little chicken, beef, pork, or seafood.

50/50— One Meal: Meatless + Vegetarian

Most of the time when I'm developing a recipe, I start by focusing on the vegetables. I come up with a plan for how I want to prepare them, I figure out what will pair well with them and what seasonings will make the dish pop, and finally I think about what meat would work well with it all. Because I think about adding meat to the dish last, it is not an integral part, and most of my recipes are as delicious and super satisfying without it as they are with it: They don't end up like a meatless Philly cheesesteak—just bread and cheese sauce (not that I wouldn't eat that, #CheeseObsessed). Even better, for these recipes it's easy to prep some portions with meat and some without it, making them particularly great for a household with a mix of those who do, and those who do not, eat meat. Spot "50/50" and you have identified one of these recipes. For many of them, you can simply omit the meat from any portions you want to be vegetarian, but if something else is needed—an extra bit of the principal vegetable or a tweak to the method—that is explained in the 50/50 tip.

FF—Family Friendly

Growing up as the pickiest of eaters, I'm aware that sometimes getting your kids to eat their veggies can be an all-out war. When the dust settles you

are probably exhausted, frustrated, and amazed at how perfectly a pea fits in your ear. But fear not, these battles can be prevented when you look for "FF," which calls out easy and delicious family-approved recipes. These include kid-friendly dishes and meals so cute they can't help but be devoured by little ones and big ones alike. Turn to these recipes when you want to expand your little ones' palates—they'll help them develop a taste for a new vegetable (or maybe even help you do the same yourself). And if a little tweaking might get a recipe to go from "yuck" to "yum," the FF tips let you know how to adjust it. Sometimes making a sauce smooth instead of chunky, hiding veggies, adding a little cheese, or reducing the spiciness can be just the thing to get the recipe ready for regular rotation in your house.

10-in-20/10-in-30—Simple + Fast

My sister's house in Buffalo always reminds me of my childhood; there are a lot of people around and there is constant action. With her four amazing children, her husband, and my mother and brother living right next door, the total number of mouths to feed on any given night hovers around eight. Throw in my other sister's family and my dad and his wife from across town, along with Lucky and Lucy (my dad's faithful companions), and you've got fifteen humans plus two pugs eager for a good meal. Cooking for this crowd when I'm visiting makes me take a step back and appreciate just how valuable easy and fast recipes can be. For me, cooking has always been about having fun, but the fun starts to feel like work when you're peeling your tenth potato or searching desperately for an ingredient you've never heard of. So when you need a meal that doesn't have a laundry list of ingredients and can be on the table quickly, look for "10-in-20" and "10-in-30." These recipes have no more than 10 ingredients and are ready in 20 or 30 minutes, making them perfect for crowds and busy nights.

500↓—Under 500 Calories

It's true, all *Meat on the Side* dishes are infinitely healthier than their meat-centric counterparts, with an average of 30 to 40 percent fewer calories and tons of extra nutrition. However, sometimes you may want a meal that's even lighter. If bathing suit season is approaching, you've had one too many Cadbury cream eggs, or you are simply counting calories, my recipes marked with "500↓" are as good for your waistline as a Zumba class. And probably better, because if you're anything like me then rhythm is not exactly your strong suit. So stop trying to channel your inner Shakira and instead whip up a 500↓ dish or two: They will help you whittle away your middle, no dancing required.

Note: Though many of my appetizers are extra lean, the 500↓ does not appear in that chapter as serving sizes vary.

Keep It Simple

Unlike baking, where using exactly the right type and amount of flour is important, cooking happily requires much less precision. The last thing I want you to do is turn away from a recipe because you don't have or don't like a particular ingredient or the recipe seems too difficult. The Keep It Simple notes that accompany many of my recipes are filled with workaround tips that make the shopping and prep easier and faster. So don't fret if you see a recipe that calls for somewhat exotic spices or vegetables that may be missing from your pantry or market; these can always be replaced with familiar and easily accessible ingredients. Plus who doesn't appreciate a shortcut or make-ahead tip? I say "Keep It Simple" by using these hints to save time and adjust the recipe so that it works for you!

Serving Suggestions!

Some of the recipes in this book, like my two tomato sauces, are basic components of other dishes. Others, like my Tiny Chicken Meatballs, are simply too scrumptious and versatile to limit to a single use. Look for the Serving Suggestions! notes to see how to mix and match these recipes with others.

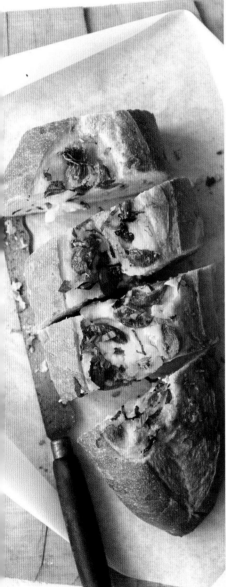

Breakfast
+ Brunch

Turnip Tortilla Pie

MAKES ONE 8-INCH PIE; SERVES 3 TO 4

500↓ | FF | 50/50

You may have seen a turnip a hundred times at the grocery store, but there is a good chance you have never actually picked up one of these white and purple striped guys, or if you have gone home with some you may have thought your only options were to keep them simple and mash or roast them. But what about creating something totally new? What about taking an omelet, stuffing it with this cabbage-like veggie and a touch of salty ham, and sandwiching it between two tortillas so you can pick it up with your hands and bite right into its eggy, hearty deliciousness? I'm calling this new thing a "Tortilla Pie"; feel free to simply call it "Awesome."

4 ounces Swiss cheese

3 teaspoons olive oil

1 small Vidalia onion, thinly sliced (about 1 cup)

1 small turnip, cut into ½-inch cubes (about 1 cup)

1¼ teaspoons kosher salt

4 large eggs

¼ cup 1 percent milk

¼ cup thinly sliced scallions, plus more for garnish

⅛ teaspoon ground black pepper

4 ounces ham, cut into ½-inch cubes (about ½ cup)

1½ cups cherry tomatoes

Two 8-inch flour tortillas

1. Preheat the oven to 350°F.

2. Shred half the cheese (to yield about ½ cup) and cut the remaining cheese into ½-inch cubes (you should have about ½ cup of these, too). Set aside.

3. Heat 2 teaspoons of the oil in an 8-inch nonstick oven-safe skillet over medium heat. Stir in the onion, turnip, and ½ teaspoon of the salt and cook, stirring occasionally, until the vegetables have softened and browned on all sides, about 15 minutes. Remove from the heat.

4. Whisk together the eggs, milk, scallions, ¼ teaspoon of the salt, and the pepper in a medium bowl until frothy and very well combined. Stir the ham and the cubed cheese into the skillet with the vegetable

mixture. Immediately pour the egg mixture over the top. Place the skillet in the oven and bake until the eggs are set and the whole mixture is firm, 25 to 30 minutes.

5. Meanwhile, toss the tomatoes with the remaining 1 teaspoon oil and the remaining ½ teaspoon salt in a medium bowl. Heat a small skillet over high heat. Add the tomatoes and cook until they burst open and become charred in spots, about 5 minutes. Set aside. Toast the tortillas by holding each with tongs over the flame of a gas burner until charred, about 10 seconds per side. If you do not have a gas stove, heat a dry medium skillet over high heat. Place the tortillas in the hot skillet, one at a time, cooking until brown spots form on the bottom, about 5 seconds. Flip and cook the opposite side in the same way.

6. Place 1 tortilla on a serving plate or cutting board and sprinkle half the shredded cheese over the top. Transfer the turnip pie onto this tortilla and sprinkle the remaining shredded cheese over it; then top it with the second tortilla. Mound the tomatoes on top, scatter with a few scallions, and cut the pie into wedges. Serve hot.

Keep It Simple

Here are some easy substitutions: Sub mozzarella or cheddar for the Swiss cheese and a white or yellow onion for the Vidalia. Replace the 1 percent milk with whole, 2 percent, or skim, and the ham with bacon or turkey. This recipe is all about using whatever you have on hand!

FF

If your kids like eggs they will love this; it's kind of a big omelet with tortillas around it. The turnips are mild in taste, but cutting them smaller can help them meld into the eggs and stay hidden.

50/50

For a half vegetarian, half meat pie, wait until the eggs are in the pan to add the ham and then sprinkle the ham over half the pie. For a totally vegetarian version you can simply omit the ham; the turnips make for a hearty pie without it.

Tomato Tart
with Gruyère + Thyme

MAKES ONE 9-INCH TART; SERVES 4

500↓ | FF | Make It Meaty

With my first garden I quickly learned that though I couldn't imagine it, those scrawny looking 1-inch tomato seedlings do in fact end up being 6 feet or taller. Along with size comes many, MANY tomatoes. This, of course, isn't a bad thing, but considering most nights it's just me and my husband at the dinner table, we suddenly had one tomato too many, or actually, twenty too many. For dinner one summer night, I knew I didn't want to shop or make anything complicated. I wanted something light, tasty, and it absolutely HAD to involve tomatoes. Well, this tart is simple, tasty, and great for breakfast, brunch, lunch, and dinner. It almost makes me wish we had more tomatoes, almost. Live, learn, and eat lots of tomatoes.

3 medium tomatoes (about 1½ pounds)

Prepared crust for one 9-inch pie (not baked)

1 tablespoon Dijon mustard

1½ cups shredded Gruyère cheese (6 ounces)

½ teaspoon kosher salt

1 teaspoon minced fresh thyme leaves

1 hot pepper (jalapeño, Fresno, or cherry pepper), seeds and ribs removed, chopped

1. Preheat the oven to 400°F.

2. Cut the tomatoes into ¼-inch-thick rounds. Take out as much of the seeds and juice as you can. Lay the rounds on paper towels and cover with more paper towels, pressing gently so the towels absorb as much moisture as possible. Repeat the process with fresh paper towels, the dryer the tomatoes the better. (If you're using heirloom tomatoes that are difficult to seed, just try to get out as much moisture as you can with the paper towels.)

3. Fit the pie crust into a 9-inch tart pan or pie plate and trim the edge even with the top of the pan. Spread the mustard evenly over the bottom of the crust and then spread the cheese over it. Arrange the

tomatoes over the cheese in a single layer (it's fine to overlap them a bit where necessary). Sprinkle the tomatoes with the salt and then the thyme. Sprinkle the chopped hot pepper over the top.

4. Bake the tart in the preheated oven until the cheese has melted, the tomatoes look slightly shriveled, and the crust is golden brown, 35 to 40 minutes. Transfer the tart to a wire rack to set for 2 to 3 minutes. Cut it into wedges and serve.

Keep It Simple

• This tart is really about using your favorite things. The Gruyère can easily be replaced with a combination of mozzarella and Parmesan, or mozzarella alone for a subtler flavor, or Parmesan alone for a more aggressive one. You can replace the thyme with your favorite herb—basil, parsley, and even rosemary are great options.
• No hot peppers around? Try sprinkling ¼ teaspoon crushed red pepper flakes over the top instead.
• Get a jump on it: Because of the baking time, technically this is not a 10-in-20 meal, but if you use premade pie crust you can whip it up, ready for the oven, in less than 10 minutes. Even better, you can put the tart together up to 6 hours ahead of time and then cover it and store in the fridge. When baking, give it an extra 5 to 10 minutes.
• Can't find a pan? Make a free-form galette (see page 189) and skip the pan entirely.

FF

Though there are some more adult flavors in this tart, they are all subtle and, at the end of the day, it's pretty much a pizza with tomatoes and cheese. Don't think the kids will go for it? Try mozzarella instead of Gruyère, skip the hot peppers, and add a little extra cheese on top of the tomatoes. They will barely even know fresh tomatoes are in there.

Make It Meaty

This is a light meal and perfect by itself or with a salad. But if you're looking for a more substantial dish, try serving it with my breaded chicken cutlets (see page 154): You can cut them up and place them on top of the tart with an extra squeeze of lemon after it has baked, or serve them on the side.

Grilled Pattypan Squash + Egg Bagel Sandwiches

MAKES 2 OPEN-FACED SANDWICHES; DOUBLE THE RECIPE AS YOU WISH

10-in-20 | 500↓ | FF | 50/50

Every morning in New York City people are enjoying bagel sandwiches. Whether with cream cheese, lox, or bacon and eggs, you really can't go wrong when layering things on a soft and chewy NYC bagel. The only thing I found missing from these iconic breakfast staples were some veggies. Lo and behold, just as I had that thought, I found a perfect, bagel-size, pattypan squash giving me the eye at the farmers' market, and I knew it was meant to be married to a bagel. If you think squash for breakfast is weird, just wait until you bite through the sweet, tender-crisp slices sitting on a throne of cheese and topped with eggs and bacon. It's going to be the new NYC breakfast staple, circa 2017!

1 pattypan squash

1 bacon strip

1 everything bagel

4 tablespoons Boursin cheese

¼ teaspoon kosher salt

⅛ teaspoon ground black pepper

1 teaspoon olive oil, plus more if needed

2 large eggs

Two 1/2-inch-thick slices large tomato (the same diameter as the bagel)

2 tablespoons finely chopped scallions

1. Trim and discard the root and vine ends of the squash. Cut two ¼-inch-thick slices crosswise from the middle section (save any scraps for another use).

2. Heat a small nonstick skillet (but large enough to fry 2 eggs) over medium heat. Add the bacon and cook until crisp, 6 to 7 minutes, turning once. Transfer the bacon to a paper towel to drain; set aside the skillet with the rendered bacon fat.

3. Meanwhile, cut the bagel in half. Spread 2 tablespoons of the cheese onto the cut side of each half and set aside.

4. Preheat a grill pan over medium-high heat. Sprinkle the squash slices on both sides with the salt and pepper and drizzle with the 1 teaspoon oil, dividing it equally. Add the squash slices to the pan and cook, turning once, until grill marks form and the squash is tender; 5 to 8 minutes.

5. While the squash cooks, heat the skillet that you cooked the bacon in over medium-low heat. If there is not enough fat in the skillet to fry the eggs, add a bit of oil. Crack the eggs into the skillet and cook to the desired doneness.

6. To assemble each sandwich, place a squash slice on top of a cheese-spread bagel half. Top it with a tomato slice and then an egg. Crumble up the bacon and scatter half on top of each sandwich, along with half the scallions. Yum!

Keep It Simple

- Pattypan squash is very similar in taste and texture to zucchini and yellow squash, so feel free to substitute slices of those when pattypan squash is not available.
- Boursin is a fabulous soft cheese made with garlic and herbs; it tastes like whipped cream cheese, which you can use instead. Regular or flavored cream cheeses will also work.
- I like to use my grill pan for this recipe as it adds a little bit of a charred flavor, but a regular skillet works just as well. This is true for most of my recipes that call for a grill pan.

FF

The squash has such a delicate flavor that it really pairs well with the bacon and eggs. In truth, it adds more texture and bite than flavor. But if your kids are not going to dig a large piece of squash on their sandwich, cut up the squash, and blend it into the cheese or scramble the eggs and fold it into them. It will be the same sandwich, but with a kid-friendly twist.

50/50

The bacon gives a nice salty flavor to the egg, but if you prefer a vegetarian version, simply omit the bacon and add a sprinkle of salt on top of your eggs. And, if you are doing one sandwich with bacon and one without, be sure to cook the second egg in a different pan. You'll have one more pan to clean, but you'll also have a happy vegetarian.

Cauliflower, Avocado + Egg Salad with Lemon Aioli

MAKES 4 SERVINGS; ABOUT 1 CUP AIOLI

10-in-20 | 500↓

Chefs like to trick you by giving fancy names to simple dishes and techniques. A favorite example is the French word "aïoli." It sounds so lovely and special, but really all it is, is garlic mayonnaise. Now don't get me wrong, a homemade mayonnaise is on a different level from the store-bought stuff—it is truly special. What? You don't think mayonnaise can be special? Well wait until you taste aioli over soft, delicate eggs with tender cauliflower and velvety avocado; you will realize just how incredibly special little old mayo can be. Go ahead, impress your friends and tell them all about this amazing dish you made with lemon aioli (and you might as well throw in a French accent when you say it).

Cauliflower, Avocado + Egg Salad

2 teaspoons kosher salt

1 medium head cauliflower (2 pounds), broken or cut into bite-size florets

4 thick slices sourdough white bread

8 hard-boiled large eggs (see Appendix, page 260)

1 avocado, pitted, peeled, and cut into ½-inch pieces

½ cup finely chopped scallions, green parts only

Chili oil (optional)

Lemon Aioli

1 large egg yolk

1 tablespoon white wine vinegar

Finely grated zest of ½ lemon

Juice of 1 lemon

1 teaspoon Dijon mustard

1 small garlic clove

1 teaspoon kosher salt

¾ cup vegetable oil

Cauliflower, Avocado + Egg Salad

1. Add ½ inch of water and 1 teaspoon of the salt to a large saucepan and bring to a boil over medium-high heat. Add the cauliflower, cover, and cook until the cauliflower is tender, 3 to 5 minutes. Drain and let cool. While the cauliflower cooks, make the Lemon Aioli (on the following page).

2. Preheat a grill pan over high heat and arrange the bread in it. Grill the bread on one side only until it is toasted and you see grill marks, 2 to 3 minutes.

3. Peel the eggs and chop them into ½-inch pieces. Put the eggs, avocados, cauliflower, and all but about 1 tablespoon of the scallions in a medium bowl and toss with the remaining 1 teaspoon salt. Add the aioli and toss to combine.

4. Place a slice of grilled bread on each of four plates. Mound the salad on top, dividing it equally. Scatter the remaining scallions over the tops, and add a few drops of chili oil to each if you wish.

Lemon Aioli

Add the egg yolk, vinegar, lemon zest, lemon juice, mustard, garlic, and salt to a blender and blend on high for 10 seconds. Leave the blender on and very slowly drizzle in the oil, starting with a couple drops and adding more as you go until the aioli has thickened. Remove from the blender and keep cold.

Keep It Simple

- The fresh aioli really gives this dish a special flavor that is delicate and indulgent at the same time, but a good-quality store-bought mayo will work fine instead: Simply add the lemon juice and garlic zest to about 1 cup mayo and mix this with the salad in step 3.
- I love to cook up several hard-boiled eggs at once; that way I can make dishes like this in the drop of a hat and I always have a great snack on hand. Keep hard-boiled eggs, in their shells, in your fridge for up to a week.
- The more oil you add to the aioli the thicker it gets. This aioli is a little thin, so if you want it thicker simply add an extra ¼ to ½ cup of oil. Add extra salt and lemon if desired.
- You can use any light-tasting vinegar in the aioli or skip it and use extra lemon juice instead.

Kale Egg Cups

MAKES 8 EGG CUPS; SERVES 4

10-in-30 | 500↓ | FF | 50/50

I've always liked cute things: kittens, tiny travel-size toiletries, my nieces in dance recitals, and, of course, I married one heck of a cute guy. And my food cannot be left off this list. I love cute food, which usually means tiny food, or individual-size eats. Considering these Kale Egg Cups literally make people stop and say "how cute," they definitely make the list. And it gets even better; not only are they cute, but they also are flavorful, healthy, and easy to whip up. You are in store for one tasty breakfast that is special enough for company and easy enough for weekday meals. And did I mention how CUTE they are?! OK, I'll stop now.

1 medium yellow onion

1 red bell pepper

4 fully cooked breakfast sausage patties

8 large kale leaves

1 tablespoon olive oil

½ teaspoon kosher salt

½ cup shredded mozzarella

8 large eggs

8 teaspoons grated Parmesan cheese

1. Preheat the oven to 375°F. Grease an 8-cup muffin pan and set the pan aside. Place a medium saucepan of water over high heat and bring to a boil.

2. Chop the onion and bell pepper and cut the sausage patties into ¼-inch pieces. Set aside.

3. One at a time, hold each kale leaf by its stem and dip it into the boiling water until it turns bright green, about 5 seconds, then lay it on some paper towels or a clean kitchen towel to drain.

4. Heat the oil in a medium skillet over medium heat. Stir in the onion, bell pepper, and salt and sauté until tender, about 5 minutes. Stir in the sausage and sauté just until it turns brown, 2 to 3 minutes more. Remove the skillet from the heat.

5. One at a time, pat each kale leaf dry with a paper towel. Cut away its stem and then cut the leaf cross-

wise into 3 pieces. Line the bottom and sides of a prepared muffin cup with the 3 pieces, overlapping them and making sure to cover the sides all the way up to the top. Repeat the procedure to line all of the cups.

6. Put 1 tablespoon of the mozzarella in each cup, top that with a spoonful of the vegetable and sausage mixture, making sure there is still room in the cup for an egg. Crack an egg into each cup and then sprinkle 1 teaspoon of the Parmesan over the egg. When all 8 cups are filled, place the muffin pan in the oven and bake until the eggs are set, 15 to 17 minutes. (Go to NikkiDinkiCooking.com for step-by-step photos.)

7. Transfer the muffin pan to a wire rack and let the egg cups cool for 2 to 3 minutes. Run a table knife around the inside edge of each cup to release anything that might be sticking. Gently lift out the kale egg cups and place 2 on each serving plate. Enjoy them hot!

FF

The cute factor of these cups is undeniable! Even if the green kale stuff might normally make your kids shy away, they will probably give them a shot.

50/50

The recipe allows half a sausage patty for each kale egg cup, so omit that amount for every cup you wish to make vegetarian. Then, when you prep the filling, remove the vegetables from the skillet before you brown the sausage; fill all the cups with the veggies and then add the sausage to whichever ones you want meat in. Figure out a way to keep track of which cups are which so you keep them separate and keep everyone happy.

Caprese Egg Boat

MAKES 2 LARGE OR 4 SMALL SERVINGS

500↓ | FF | Make It Meaty

Good bread is always nice just for nibbling, but it can also be transformed into a super-simple and yet applause-worthy breakfast. And if you have a forgotten loaf, then no problem, this recipe can bring it back to its glory days. So take that baguette, sourdough, or Pullman loaf, cut it open, stuff it with eggs, some cheese, tomatoes, and basil and watch as the baking eggs soak into the bread and become something much more than just eggs and bread.

1 medium bread loaf

4 large eggs

¼ cup heavy cream

1 tablespoon finely chopped basil leaves, plus more for garnish

1 teaspoon kosher salt

¼ teaspoon ground black pepper

½ cup halved grape tomatoes

½ cup cubed fresh mozzarella cheese (½-inch cubes)

1. Preheat the oven to 325°F.

2. Cut an oval hollow into the top of the bread, using a serrated knife, leaving a border of ½ to 1 inch all around. Scoop out the inside and reserve it for another use. Transfer to a baking dish.

3. Whisk together the eggs, cream, basil, salt, and pepper in a medium bowl. Fold in the tomatoes and mozzarella. Pour the mixture into the hollow in the bread.

4. Bake the filled bread until the eggs are set and the filling is firm (press lightly with your fingers to test), 45 to 50 minutes. Transfer the baking dish to a wire rack and let rest for 3 to 5 minutes. Cut crosswise into 2-inch-thick slices, scatter some minced basil on top, and serve.

Mushroom Breakfast Polenta

MAKES 2 HEARTY SERVINGS OR 4 LIGHTER ONES

50/50

I don't have to write much here to sell you on this dish. It is warm and cheesy polenta, topped with browned shiitakes, a hint of herb, sausage, a poached egg, and a drizzle of maple syrup. And it's as good at 8 PM as it is at 8 AM. Really what more could you want?!

4 country white bread slices, plus more if you like

4 cups water

¾ cup medium-ground polenta or cornmeal

2½ teaspoons kosher salt

5 tablespoons (½ stick plus 1 tablespoon) unsalted butter

¾ cup grated Parmesan cheese (3 ounces), plus more for garnish

4 fully cooked breakfast sausage patties

1 pound shiitake mushrooms, stems removed, caps cut into ½-inch-thick slices

¼ cup finely chopped scallions, green parts only, plus more for garnish

1 teaspoon minced fresh rosemary leaves

1 tablespoon sherry vinegar

1 tablespoon white vinegar

4 large eggs

¼ cup maple syrup

1. Preheat a grill pan over high heat. Working in batches if necessary, arrange the bread slices in the pan in a single layer and grill until they are lightly toasted and you see grill marks, 1 to 2 minutes per side.

2. Bring 3 cups of water to a simmer in a medium saucepan. Gradually whisk in the polenta and let it simmer until soft and thick, 18 to 20 minutes, whisking frequently. If it gets really stiff, whisk in more simmering water, ¼ cup at a time, whisking each addition until fully incorporated before adding more. When the polenta has a consistency you like, whisk in 1½ teaspoons of the salt and then stir in 2 tablespoons of the butter and the Parmesan until blended. Cover and keep warm.

3. While the polenta cooks, prepare the sausage and mushrooms: Heat a large skillet over medium-high heat. Add the sausage in a single layer and cook until browned on both sides, 1 to 2 minutes per side. Transfer the sausage to paper towels to drain. Melt the remaining 3 tablespoons butter in the same skillet. Stir in the mushrooms and cook, without stirring, until their undersides are dark brown, about 2 minutes.

Stir in the scallions, rosemary, sherry vinegar, and remaining 1 teaspoon salt and cook until the mushrooms are tender, 2 to 3 minutes more. Return the sausage to the skillet and keep everything warm while you poach the eggs.

4. Add 2 to 3 inches of water to a large saucepan or large deep skillet and bring to a boil. Reduce the heat and adjust to maintain a slow simmer (where just a couple of bubbles form). Add the white vinegar. Crack an egg into a small bowl or a coffee cup and then slide it into the water; repeat right away with each remaining egg. Cook the eggs until the whites are firm but the yolks are still soft, 4 to 6 minutes. Using a slotted spoon, transfer the eggs to paper towels to drain.

5. To serve, spoon the polenta into shallow bowls. Top each serving with some sausage, mushrooms, an egg, a drizzle of maple syrup, and a scattering of chopped scallions. Pass additional Parmesan and the grilled bread at the table.

Keep It Simple

- Using quick-cooking polenta will save time, but some people find it has less texture and taste than regular polenta.
- Shiitake mushrooms have a nice, rich mushroom flavor, but similarly rich mushrooms like portobellos, cremini, or chanterelles would all make for a fantastic dish.
- Sherry vinegar is a little musty and pairs nicely with the mushrooms; however red wine vinegar, white wine vinegar, or even balsamic will all work fine.

50/50

Since the polenta and egg are both hearty and satisfying, the sausage here is really optional and can be easily omitted to create vegetarian portions. Or if you prefer, add an extra egg to the meatless portions.

Potato + Parsnip Hash Browns
with Sriracha Ketchup

MAKES 2 HEARTY SERVINGS OR 4 LIGHTER ONE; ABOUT 1 CUP KETCHUP

10-in-20 | FF | 500↓

For the start of seventh grade, I decided that I needed a special outfit that would make me stand out, make me sparkle! Considering our family's tight budget this was going to have to be of the homemade variety. I smothered some old sneakers in glue and dipped them in silver sparkles. Suddenly my "same-old" sneakers were SPECIAL. This same idea can go for your food. You probably have classic hash browns all the time. But try grating in a little parsnip and jazzing up your ketchup with sriracha and orange: You suddenly have something special. It may not be as special as my sparkly shoes, but it's a very close second and it doesn't leave a trail of silver sparkles wherever you go.

Sriracha Ketchup

1 cup ketchup

1 tablespoon sriracha sauce

Finely grated zest of 1 orange

Potato + Parsnip Hash Browns

2 small Idaho potatoes (about 1 pound), peeled and grated

1 large parsnip (about ½ pound), grated

1 tablespoon olive oil

½ teaspoon kosher salt

⅛ teaspoon ground black pepper

Sriracha Ketchup

Whisk together the ketchup, sriracha, and orange zest in a small bowl, blending well.

Potato + Parsnip Hash Browns

1. Spread out the grated potatoes and parsnips on a clean kitchen towel or piece of cheesecloth, roll up the

towel, and then wring out as much liquid from the vegetables as possible. This is very important; you want them to be as dry as possible so wring out as much of their liquid as you can.

2. Heat the oil in a large skillet over medium-high heat. Shake the vegetables out of the towel into a medium bowl and mix them with the salt and pepper. Spread them out in a layer or free-form patties in the hot pan and let them cook, undisturbed, until browned on the bottom, about 4 minutes. Flip them over and cook until browned on the opposite side, 4 minutes more. Serve immediately, with the Sriracha Ketchup on the side.

Keep It Simple

• Use any hot sauce you like in the ketchup, and use more or less depending on how spicy you like things.

• For a different spin, you can grate up a carrot or a turnip instead of the parsnip.

FF

• These hash browns are a great way to shake things up at the breakfast table and get some extra veggies into your meal. The parsnips add a subtle flavor and completely blend in color-wise.

• Go light on the sriracha for young kids, or leave it out. These hash browns are also great with my BBQ sauce (see page 213).

MY ONE TRUE LOVE, THE FOOD PROCESSOR

I'm slightly obsessed with my food processor. Though I don't like to pick favorites in my kitchen, I have to make the other appliances jealous and say it's by far my favorite piece of equipment. It mixes, it purees, it chops, it grates, and it's half the size of my stand mixer. This size difference becomes very important when you live in a city like New York, a place where many people keep things in places they don't belong, like sweaters in their ovens. While my sweaters are cozy in my dresser and not in any risk of getting baked or broiled, my mixer does get stuffed into my linen closet. Every time I go to use it I have to debate if it's really worth digging it out and lugging it to the kitchen. The majority of the time I decide to just dump whatever it is in my much more accessible food processor and see what happens instead. And what makes me even happier is that I can slip all the attachments in the dishwasher in the end. It's the little things that really make my day, and no chopping paired with an easy cleanup always make for a great day.

Zucchini Quiche
with Potato Crust

MAKES ONE 9-INCH QUICHE; SERVES 4 TO 6

500↓ | FF | 50/50

My husband and I had our first date at a French bistro in our neighborhood. Eleven years later the restaurant is still one of our favorite spots. It is dimly lit, noisy, bustling, the wine flows like water—and they have a quiche du jour. Even my husband, who loves their steak and duck, finds himself drawn to their classic French quiches, which are rich yet light and great at any hour. So I challenged myself to echo that bistro quiche and bring the good times home: With a little fontina cheese for creaminess, bacon for a salty kick, and a spiced potato crust that is firm yet chewy, this is good enough to be the quiche du jour every day.

Potato Crust

1 large Idaho potato (about 1 pound)

1 cup all-purpose flour

1 large egg

1 teaspoon kosher salt

¼ teaspoon garlic powder

¼ teaspoon dried oregano

Zucchini Filling

2 bacon strips

Olive oil, if needed

1 medium zucchini (about ½ pound), finely chopped

¾ teaspoon kosher salt

4 large eggs

¾ cup milk

1 scallion, thinly sliced

2 ounces shredded Gruyère cheese

Potato Crust

1. Preheat the oven to 400°F. Grease a 9-inch pie plate.

2. Peel the potatoes and then grate them on the large holes on a box grater or with the grating attachment on your food processor; you should have 3 cups. Add the potatoes, flour, egg, salt, garlic powder, and

oregano to a large bowl and stir until well combined. Press the mixture over the bottom and up the sides of the prepared pie plate. Bake the crust until firm and lightly brown around the edges, about 30 minutes.

Zucchini Filling

1. While the crust is baking, heat a large skillet over medium heat. Add the bacon and cook until crisp, 6 to 7 minutes, turning once. Transfer the bacon to a paper towel to drain. If there is not enough bacon fat in the skillet to sauté the zucchini, add a bit of oil and heat it briefly. Stir in the zucchini and ¼ teaspoon of the salt and cook until the zucchini is crisp-tender, about 5 minutes. Set the zucchini aside to cool slightly.

2. When the crust is nearly done, chop the bacon. Whisk together the eggs, milk, and sliced scallion in a large bowl until blended. Stir in the zucchini, bacon, Gruyère, and the remaining ½ teaspoon salt and mix well. Remove the baked crust from the oven, pour the filling mixture into it, and return it to the oven and bake until the filling is set in the center (press gently with your finger to test), about 30 minutes. Serve the quiche hot and delicious, cut into wedges.

FF

Most kids are on board with a meal that's got potato, eggs, and bacon. But if the zucchini is really a problem, leave it out. You can sub in their favorite veggie, or make the crust using equal parts sweet potato and Idaho potato so it's a nutrient-rich dish even without the veggie in the filling.

50/50

To make this half vegetarian use only 1 strip of bacon and cook it in a separate pan from the zucchini. Don't mix the bacon into the filling, instead, once the filling is poured over the potato crust sprinkle the bacon over half of the quiche and then bake as instructed. Or if you prefer, use 2 mini pie pans and make a nonbacon version in one.

Tomatoes

There is literally nothing better than walking outside on a sunny summer morning, picking a perfectly ripe tomato off the vine, and then slicing it superthin, layering it on toast, and topping it with eggs. Tomatoes were the first vegetable that I learned to enjoy. The tomato originally came from South America and was at one time thought to be poisonous (when I was a kid I also thought this). But once our forefathers realized that the tomato was actually sweet, perfectly acidic, and juicy, they were hooked. I like my tomatoes raw, roasted, sauced, pickled, broiled, fried, and grilled. I like them to star in a recipe and I like them in supporting roles. I guess what I'm trying to say is, I sure like tomatoes.

Recipe List

Peppers + Chiles

Bell peppers are a great source of 30 different carotenoids (which include alpha-carotene and beta-carotene) and have all the vitamin C you could need. And hot peppers, often called chiles, have all that plus they put your metabolism into high gear. All peppers start out green, but the riper they are the more colorful they get (think red, orange, and yellow) and the more nutritious they become. But that doesn't mean that green peppers, especially the sweet bell peppers, should be ignored. You can usually find them for less than half the price of their colorful sisters, so I like to load up and make them into things like taco fillings and appetizers. And I save the sweeter ones for pureeing into sauces or serving raw. And, of course, a spicy chile like a jalapeño or poblano pops up in my appetizers and on my pizzas when I look for heat and also big flavor. You think you like peppers already?! Well now you're about to become obsessed.

Recipe List

Tomato + Strawberry French Toast
with Maple–Cream Cheese Icing

MAKES 8 SLICES TOAST; ABOUT ½ CUP ICING

—

FF

At this point we all know that a tomato is technically a fruit, but do we really believe that it is? I first served this dish at an event where many questioned the place tomatoes had sitting next to strawberries atop their French toast. It's human nature to question things, and it can also be human nature to be afraid of new things. But sometimes if we stop asking so many questions, stop analyzing everything, and just dig in and eat the darn thing, we would realize just how good something like this is. We would see how an ever-so slightly acidic tomato brightens up and complements sweet food. Still don't believe me? OK, be here in five; I'm making you French toast.

Maple–Cream Cheese Icing

2 tablespoons unsalted butter, at room temperature

2 ounces cream cheese, at room temperature

⅓ cup powdered sugar

2 tablespoons maple syrup

¼ teaspoon vanilla extract

Strawberry French Toast

1 cup quartered grape tomatoes

1 cup quartered strawberries

2 teaspoons granulated sugar

1 cup half-and-half

3 large eggs

2 tablespoons honey

1 teaspoon ground cinnamon

Pinch of ground nutmeg

½ teaspoon kosher salt

Eight ¾-inch-thick slices challah,
    or other white bread

1 tablespoon unsalted butter

Chopped fresh mint leaves, for serving

Maple–Cream Cheese Icing

Using an electric mixer on high speed, beat the butter and cream cheese until combined. Turn the mixer to low and beat in the powdered sugar, maple syrup, and vanilla, beating until a smooth icing forms. Set aside while you make the French toast.

Strawberry French Toast

1. Put the tomatoes, strawberries, and granulated sugar in a medium bowl and gently stir together.

2. Whisk together the half-and-half, eggs, honey, cinnamon, nutmeg, and salt in a large bowl until well combined. Submerge the bread slices in the egg mixture and let them soak for at least 2 minutes.

3. Heat a large skillet or griddle over medium-low heat. Melt the butter in the pan, spreading it evenly over the surface. Working in batches if necessary, arrange the bread slices in the pan and cook until golden brown on both sides and firm in the middle, 2 to 3 minutes per side.

4. To serve, place 2 slices of toast on each plate. Spoon the tomatoes and strawberries over them. Drizzle or spread the icing on top (you can put it in a squeeze bottle if you want to get a piped effect) and sprinkle with some chopped mint.

Keep It Simple

- I like half-and-half in this recipe because it creates a thick and rich custard; alternatively, you could use heavy cream for a similar consistency. Considering you've got a killer icing on this French toast, you could instead lighten things up a bit by using buttermilk, 2 percent, or 1 percent milk.
- The nutmeg gives a touch of warmth to the French toast, but it is totally optional; don't worry if you don't have any or don't like it.
- Grape tomatoes work best for this as they are generally extra sweet, and as this is a sweeter dish you don't want a tomato that's too acidic.

FF

French toast with a serving of veggies, what more could you ask for? The quartered tomatoes blend in really well with the strawberries, but if you're afraid your kids will pick them out, try finely chopping the strawberries and tomatoes: they will just see red deliciousness and won't think twice. A little extra icing is always a hit, too.

Pumpkin Pancakes +
Easy Salted Caramel Sauce

MAKES 12 MINI PANCAKES, 1½ CUPS SAUCE, AND 2 CUPS WHIPPED CREAM

—

FF

Some of my best memories are of working with my sister Alecia at a diner back in Buffalo. We served a lot of pancakes there, but somehow I never really got their immense appeal. I've always wanted more from my pancakes: more dimension, more fun, and now, more veggies. These pumpkin pancakes give you all that! With the addition of salted caramel and whipped cream, you might as well stick a candle in this stack and call it a birthday cake. Happy birthday to YOU!

Easy Salted Caramel Sauce

1 cup packed brown sugar (light or dark)

½ cup heavy cream

4 tablespoons (½ stick) unsalted butter,
    cut into pieces

1 teaspoon vanilla extract

1 teaspoon kosher salt

Whipped Cream

1 cup heavy cream, very cold

1 teaspoon vanilla extract

2 tablespoons powdered sugar

Pumpkin Pancakes

1¼ cups all-purpose flour

3 tablespoons granulated sugar

2 teaspoons baking powder

½ teaspoon ground cinnamon

¼ teaspoon ground allspice

¼ teaspoon ground ginger

¼ teaspoon kosher salt

Pinch of ground nutmeg

3 tablespoons unsalted butter

1¼ cups whole milk

¾ cup 100 percent pure pumpkin puree

1 large egg

Easy Salted Caramel Sauce

Add the brown sugar, cream, and butter to a medium saucepan. Place over medium heat and cook, stirring often, until the sugar has dissolved and the butter has melted. Continue cooking until the sauce has thickened, 5 to 7 minutes. Remove the pan from the heat and stir in the vanilla and salt. Keep warm over low heat so you can serve the sauce hot when the pancakes are ready.

Whipped Cream

Put the cream, vanilla, and powdered sugar in the bowl of a mixer fitted with the whisk attachment. Turn the mixer to high speed and whisk the cream until soft peaks form, 1 to 2 minutes. Refrigerate the whipped cream, covered, until ready to serve.

Pumpkin Pancakes

1. Whisk together the flour, granulated sugar, baking powder, cinnamon, allspice, ginger, salt, and nutmeg in a large bowl. Put 2 tablespoons of the butter in a small microwave-safe bowl and microwave on high for 30 seconds until melted. In a second medium bowl, whisk together the milk, pumpkin, and egg; then whisk in the melted butter. Add the milk mixture to the flour mixture and stir just until combined; some lumps are OK.

2. Preheat the oven to 200°F. Heat a large skillet or griddle over medium heat. Melt the remaining 1 tablespoon butter in the skillet, spreading it evenly over the surface. Working in batches as necessary, ladle ¼-cup portions of the batter onto the skillet, spacing them a little apart. Cook the pancakes until they are golden brown on both sides and cooked through, 2 to 3 minutes per side. Keep the first batch warm in the oven while you cook the second batch.

3. To serve, divide the pancakes among individual plates. Pour the warm caramel sauce over each serving and top with a dollop of whipped cream.

Keep It Simple

- Replace the spices with 1¼ teaspoons pumpkin pie spice mix. Do this and you can count the pancake part of this as a 10-in-20 recipe.
- Starting with ready-made whipped cream and caramel sauce makes for a super-speedy brunch treat. Just add a touch of salt to the store-bought caramel for a similar effect.
- The amount of liquid in canned pumpkin puree can vary by brand. If you feel your pancake batter is too thick, simply stir in a touch more milk.

Appetizers
+ Nibblers

Dips

French Onion Soup Dip

MAKES ABOUT 2 CUPS DIP

—

FF

One of my absolute favorite soups is French Onion. With its intensely sweet caramelized onions, rich broth, and mounds of melted cheese, it's a soup that no one can resist. So why not take these flavors and twist them into an equally incredible appetizer? It's just as good as the original dish, with bubbling cheese and rich flavors, but it's spreadable. Who could want anything more?!

2 tablespoons unsalted butter

3 pounds Vidalia onions, thinly sliced

1 teaspoon kosher salt

2 garlic cloves, minced

2 bay leaves

2 teaspoons minced fresh thyme leaves

1 teaspoon sugar

½ cup beef stock

2 cups shredded Gruyère cheese (8 ounces)

Crackers or baguette slices, for serving

1. Melt the butter in a large skillet over medium-high heat. Add the onions and salt and cook, stirring frequently, until the onions stop releasing water and there is little to no liquid in the skillet, about 20 minutes. The onions should have no color at this point so adjust the heat accordingly. Reduce the heat to medium and continue to cook the onions, stirring only occasionally, until they begin to caramelize and turn medium brown, about 30 minutes.

2. Reduce the heat to medium-low and stir in the garlic, bay leaves, thyme, and sugar. Continue to cook, stirring only occasionally, until the onions are a deep brown color all over, about 20 minutes more. Stir in the stock, scraping with a wooden spoon to release any brown bits stuck to the bottom of the skillet. Cook until most of the liquid is absorbed; remove and discard the bay leaves. Add 1½ cups of the cheese and stir until combined. Transfer the onion mixture to a small casserole or oven-safe bowl.

3. Place a rack in the broiler sufficiently below the heat source to accommodate the casserole, and turn on the broiler. Scatter the remaining ½ cup cheese evenly over the top of the onion mixture in the casserole. Broil until the cheese is melted and bubbling. Serve immediately, accompanied by the crackers or baguette slices and a small knife for spreading.

Beet Hummus

MAKES 2½ CUPS HUMMUS

—

FF

I had one week between finding out I was chosen to be on *Food Network Star* and getting on the plane to LA. In that time I tried to cram as much info into my head as I possibly could. I made flash cards of favorite recipes, asked myself what I would do in situations other chefs had faced in past seasons, and tested some recipe ideas that were floating in my head that I thought were show-worthy, like this beet hummus. I knew that by adding beets to a hummus I would end up with fantastic flavor *and* showstopping color. Though I never got to make this on the show, it is definitely worthy to be on TV and also on your table.

3 medium red beets (about ¾ pound combined)

2 garlic cloves

One 15-ounce can chickpeas, rinsed and drained

2 tablespoons tahini paste

1½ teaspoons kosher salt, plus more if needed

½ teaspoon ground cumin

½ teaspoon ground coriander

¼ cup sour cream

⅓ cup lightly packed fresh flat-leaf parsley leaves, plus more for garnish (optional)

⅓ cup extra-virgin olive oil

½ cup pomegranate seeds (see Appendix, page 261)

Pita chips, for serving

1. Preheat the oven to 375°F.

2. Wrap the beets (all together) in aluminum foil and bake them until you can easily insert a fork into the center of the flesh, 45 to 60 minutes. The time can vary greatly depending on the size of your beets, but the good news is that overbaking them won't hurt them at all. Immediately remove the skin from the beets by rubbing each with paper towels.

3. Put the beets and garlic in a food processor and process until finely chopped. Add the chickpeas, tahini, salt, cumin, and coriander and process again until finely chopped. Spoon in the sour cream and

Broccoli + Feta Dip

Beet Hummus
(p. 37)

parsley and then, with the machine running, drizzle in the oil, processing until you get a smooth and slightly creamy mixture. Taste the hummus and add up to another ½ teaspoon of salt if you wish.

4. Transfer the hummus to a small serving bowl and fold in the pomegranate seeds. Top with some extra chopped parsley if you wish. Serve with pita chips on the side.

Keep It Simple

• Pressed for time? Many grocery stores now sell cooked, peeled beets in packages. Look for them in the produce section, then you can whip this hummus up in 10 minutes or less! You can also peel and chop whole raw beets into smaller pieces before baking to cut down on cooking time significantly.

• Season to taste: You can use just cumin, just coriander, or both as the recipe suggests.

• Tahini is a paste of ground sesame seeds. If you can't find it, use almond butter. Or in a pinch, try 1 tablespoon peanut butter along with an extra 2 tablespoons olive oil.

FF

Kids like hummus? But not beet hummus? Use golden yellow beets instead of red for a much less alarming color. And if they are just getting used to the flavor of beets, use half the amount of beets that the recipe calls for along with ¼ teaspoon less salt.

Broccoli + Feta Dip

MAKES 2 CUPS DIP

10-in-20 | FF

In this dip, the feta is so rich and tangy and gets along great with the broccoli, which sneaks in just a touch of much-needed bitterness. Finish with some mint and a little peppery heat, and you will want to spread this on absolutely everything. Yep, even your shoe would taste good with this dip, but for now, lets just stick to a cracker.

2 cups broccoli florets (about ½ pound broccoli)

1 hot pepper or ¼ teaspoon crushed red pepper flakes, plus more as needed and for garnish

1 garlic clove

½ teaspoon kosher salt, plus more as needed

7 ounces feta cheese

¼ cup extra-virgin olive oil

Finely grated zest and juice of 1 lemon

2 tablespoons chopped fresh mint leaves, plus more for garnish (or basil or thyme)

Crackers, pita chips, or baguette slices, for serving

1. Bring a large pot of salted water to a boil over high heat. Add the broccoli and cook until it is slightly tender and bright green, about 3 minutes. Drain the broccoli and run cold water over it until it is cool.

2. Put the broccoli, hot pepper, garlic, and salt in a food processor and pulse 10 times until everything is coarsely chopped. Add the feta, oil, lemon zest, lemon juice, and mint and pulse several times until everything is finely chopped and the mixture comes together as a dip. Taste the dip and add more salt if desired. Check the heat, too—add more hot pepper if you want your dip spicier.

3. Serve garnished with a bit of chopped hot pepper and crackers on the side.

FF

You can easily get away with selling this as a cheese dip to your kids, keeping the broccoli part to yourself. And if you think a little green will throw them off, swap the broccoli for cauliflower and watch them gobble it up!

Cabbage Nachos
with Tomatillo Salsa

MAKES 1 LARGE PLATE OF NACHOS

10-in-30 | FF | Make It Meaty

My husband and I watch football every Sunday, and sometimes to my dismay, Thursday, Saturday, and Monday, too. I like football, but I like football food even better. A football game is a good excuse to whip up snacks, open some beers, or maybe some sparkling rosé, and watch TV all day. But how do you make tailgate foods into *Meat on the Side* staples? Easy, you take something like nachos and add cabbage of course. It works—really!! Mild, crunchy cabbage adds texture and acts as a delicious glue to hold a showstopping tomatillo salsa and crispy chip together. Bring on the football!! Just maybe not SO much football.

¾ pound tomatillos (5 to 7), husks removed

1 fresh jalapeño or serrano chile

½ yellow onion, peeled and cut into 4 wedges

2 tablespoons olive oil

3 teaspoons kosher salt

½ cup loosely packed fresh cilantro leaves

5 cups lightly packed shredded green cabbage
 (about half a head)

30 large tortilla chips

2 cups shredded Pepper Jack cheese (8 ounces)

¼ cup pickled sliced jalapeño chiles

1. Turn on the broiler to high, if you have that option. Place the tomatillos, fresh jalapeño, and onion wedges on a rimmed baking sheet, drizzle with 1 tablespoon of the oil, and stir to coat the vegetables. Broil until the vegetables are tender and slightly charred, 7 to 10 minutes. (You may have to remove the tomatillos and jalapeños and let the onions cook for an extra minute or so.) Leave the broiler on while you do the next steps.

2. To make the salsa, transfer the charred vegetables to a food processor or blender and add 2 teaspoons of the salt and the cilantro. Process until almost smooth.

3. Heat the remaining 1 tablespoon oil in a medium skillet over medium heat. Stir in the cabbage and remaining 1 teaspoon salt and cook until the cabbage is tender but not mushy, about 5 minutes. Remove the skillet from the heat and stir in about half the salsa until combined. You want the cabbage to be coated, but not dripping wet, so stir in as much of the rest of the salsa as you need to get to that point.

4. Arrange the tortilla chips in a single layer on a large oven-safe serving dish. Spread the cabbage mixture over the chips and then sprinkle the cheese evenly over the top. Broil the nachos until the cheese has melted and is bubbling. Scatter the pickled jalapeños over the top and serve right away.

Keep It Simple

- Tomatillos look like green tomatoes with papery skins around them, they are slightly denser than tomatoes and taste like a tart apple. If you're having trouble finding them at your store, you can use tomatoes instead—the taste will be different but similarly delicious.
- To make this dish in less than 10 minutes, try these shortcuts: simply buy a jar of your favorite green or red salsa instead of making the tomatillo salsa. And save major time by purchasing shredded cabbage or coleslaw mix as well as shredded cheese at your market; no need to do it yourself!

FF

Your family will never know there is a pound of cabbage sitting in these nachos. The sautéed cabbage has a really mild flavor and its job is to help the tomatillo salsa stay on the nachos to give you a flavorful hit with every bite.

Make It Meaty

These nachos are currently meatless, but you can add your favorite nacho topping, including ground beef, over the whole plate—or just over half for a 50/50 appetizer.

Broccoli Dippers

MAKES AN APPETIZER FOR 4

10-in-20 | FF

We've all been to that party: You show up starving and the only thing to satisfy the hungry monster that recently relocated to your belly is a crudité platter of raw broccoli sitting around a bowl of some ranchlike dressing. If only your host had read this incredible new cookbook called *Meat on the Side*, she would have realized that in 20 minutes she could create something that celebrates broccoli, enhancing it with spice, and pairing it with a sinfully delicious chipotle-studded cheese sauce. Don't worry, you may be stuck at this party right now, but as soon as you get home, you are whipping up these Broccoli Dippers and not sharing with anyone.

1 large head broccoli

2 tablespoons olive oil

1 teaspoon kosher salt

1 teaspoon paprika, plus more for garnish

½ teaspoon garlic powder

1 tablespoon unsalted butter

1 tablespoon all-purpose flour

½ cup whole milk

1 cup shredded extra-sharp cheddar cheese
   (4 ounces)

¼ cup grated Parmesan cheese (1 ounce)

1½ teaspoons chipotle puree (page 259)

1. Preheat the oven to 400°F. Separate the top of the broccoli into large florets; leave about an inch of the little branch part on each floret so you have something to hold when you dip it. Toss with the oil, salt, paprika, and garlic powder in a large bowl until well coated. Spread on a rimmed baking sheet and bake until tender but firm, 10 to 15 minutes.

2. Meanwhile, make the cheese sauce: Melt the butter in a small saucepan over medium heat. Whisk in the flour and cook for 1 minute. Whisk in the milk and continue whisking until there are no lumps. Cook, whisking occasionally, until the mixture has bubbled and thickened, 3 to 5 minutes. Add the cheeses, ½ cup at a time, whisking well until each addition has melted and incorporated. Stir in the chipotle puree.

3. To serve, transfer the cheese sauce to a small bowl, sprinkle some paprika over the top, and place on a platter. Arrange the broccoli around it, or in a shallow dish, and dip away!

Crab-Stuffed Endive

MAKES 8 STUFFED LEAVES

10-in-20

Every New Year's Eve my mom and dad would splurge on crab legs. None of us kids got any, not that we would go near them, and the two of them sat there cracking away having their New Year's Eve in style. So when my dad visited New York City and we had a big dinner on my terrace, I knew getting some crab involved would make the evening truly special. I brought out this perfect bite of crab. Light yet creamy, bright and complex, with crispy and bitter endive holding it all together. It may not have been New Year's Eve 1991, but it was surely a night to remember.

Juice of ½ lemon

1 ounce cream cheese, at room temperature

1 tablespoon mayonnaise

2 teaspoons champagne vinegar

1 teaspoon kosher salt

½ teaspoon smoked paprika

1½ cups finely chopped frisée lettuce

½ red bell pepper, seeded and finely chopped

6 ounces lump crabmeat, drained if canned

8 large Belgian endive leaves (from 1 or 2 heads as needed)

1 tablespoon finely chopped fresh chives

1. Blend the lemon juice, cream cheese, mayonnaise, vinegar, salt, and paprika in a medium bowl. Add the chopped frisée and bell pepper and stir until well combined. Add the crabmeat and stir gently just until incorporated; you don't want to break it up too much.

2. Spoon the crab mixture into the hollow of each endive leaf; sprinkle the chives over the endive and serve.

Keep It Simple

• Fresh and canned crabmeat work equally well in this delicious recipe, so use whichever is easiest. Look for lump crabmeat near the seafood counter, buy some crabs and pick your own meat, or look for a good-quality canned variety and drain it before using.

• To save time, serve the stuffing in a bowl with crackers instead of in the endive leaves.

• If you like, substitute white wine vinegar for the champagne vinegar.

Broiled Feta + Hot Pepper Relish

MAKES AN APPETIZER FOR 6

10-in-20

The first year of my Manhattan terrace garden was a bit experimental. I planted almost sixty different things, from tomatoes to kohlrabi to lemongrass. When I took stock at the end of the season one thing was for sure: I was going to grow A LOT of peppers next time. They were by far the easiest plants to take care of and the rainbow harvest of hot and sweet peppers was incredible. And they made the most amazing dish—this relish with sun-dried tomatoes and feta, bursting with an array of smoky, sweet, and spicy peppers.

1 small banana pepper, seeded and chopped

1 orange bell pepper, cored, seeded, and chopped

½ poblano chile, seeds and ribs removed, chopped

1 serrano or habanero chile, seeds and ribs removed, chopped

1 garlic clove

⅓ cup sun-dried tomatoes, drained

½ teaspoon kosher salt

1 tablespoon olive oil

One 6-ounce brick feta cheese, drained and patted dry

Toasted baguette slices or crackers, for serving

1. Put the peppers, chiles, garlic, tomatoes, and salt in a food processor. Pulse until finely chopped.

2. Heat the oil in a small skillet over medium heat. Add the pepper-chile mixture and cook until everything is tender, about 5 minutes.

3. Spread the mixture in a small casserole, covering the bottom. Center the cheese on top. Position a rack in the broiler sufficiently below the heat source to accommodate the casserole. Turn on the broiler, to high if you have that option. Broil until the cheese is brown on top and the pepper-chile mixture is slightly charred, about 5 minutes. Serve immediately, with the bread on the side.

Keep It Simple

Use whatever peppers and chiles you have on hand or whatever ones you love the most.

Pumpkin Poppers

MAKES 40 TO 48 POPPERS

10-in-30 | FF

My brother-in-law Josh is a "Meat in the Middle" kind of guy. So when I visit I try to make things he will love, but that stay true to my Meat on the Side point of view. These Pumpkin Poppers totally fit the bill, with chorizo for big flavor and pumpkin and spices that linger delightfully in your mouth.

2 links chorizo (4 ounces each)

One 15-ounce can 100 percent pure pumpkin puree

4 ounces soft goat cheese

1 teaspoon kosher salt

1 tablespoon chopped fresh sage

2 tablespoons finely chopped fresh chives

Pinch of ground nutmeg

Two 8-ounce cans crescent roll dough

1. Preheat the oven to 350°F. Place a large skillet over medium heat. Remove the casing from the sausage and add the meat to the skillet. Cook for about 4 minutes, breaking the meat apart into small pieces with a spoon as it cooks. Reduce the heat to low, add the pumpkin, cheese, and salt, and stir until the cheese has melted, about 2 minutes. Turn off the heat and stir in the sage, chives, and nutmeg. Transfer the filling mixture to a plate and refrigerate to cool slightly while you prepare the dough.

2. Grease two mini muffin pans. Unroll the dough from one can onto a lightly floured surface. With your fingers, pinch together the dough along the perforations dividing the rolls, so the sheet holds together. Then roll out the dough into a rectangle that is about 12 × 18-inches. Using a sharp knife, cut the rectangle into 24 squares, making 5 cuts crosswise and 3 cuts lengthwise. Separate the squares and place each one into a muffin cup. Repeat this process with the dough from the second can.

3. Spoon 2 teaspoons of the filling into the center of each square. Fold the dough corners over, enclosing the filling. Bake the poppers until the dough is golden brown, about 15 minutes. Serve hot!

Keep It Simple

• Chorizo has big flavor and adds a lot to this dish, but feel free to use your favorite sausage.

Mushroom Pâté
Crostini (p. 53)

Zucchini Crostini
with Pomegranate–
Goat Cheese Spread
(p. 57)

Spicy Green Pepper
+ Edamame Crostini (p. 55)

Crostinis

Mushroom Pâté Crostini

MAKES 20 CROSTINI

50/50

The technical definition of the term *pâté* is cooked meat and fat minced until a paste forms. So, it seems as though I have lied to you once again. Yes, this recipe is not really a pâté, BUT it looks like pâté and it tastes like pâté. And for good measure there is a touch of bacon on top, so there is some meat in this recipe, just not quite as much as the original. See, I like to play with traditional recipes and put my spin on them, taking things that are always done one way and doing them the "wrong" way. So maybe this is a pâté or perhaps a "pâté," but either way it's darn tasty.

4 ounces Parmesan cheese

10 cornichons

1 baguette, cut into twenty ¼-inch-thick slices

1 tablespoon extra-virgin olive oil

10 ounces baby bella mushrooms, stems discarded, caps coarsely chopped

4 ounces shiitake mushrooms, stems discarded, caps coarsely chopped

4 garlic cloves, minced

½ teaspoon kosher salt

2 tablespoons dry Marsala wine

1 teaspoon fresh rosemary leaves, minced

1 teaspoon fresh thyme leaves

1 tablespoon truffle oil

1 cup shredded Gruyère cheese (4 ounces)

2 bacon strips

1. Grate enough of the Parmesan to equal ½ cup, cover, and set aside. Shave the remaining Parmesan with a vegetable peeler, cover, and set aside. Slice the cornichons into thin rounds, cover, and set aside.

2. Preheat a grill pan over high heat. Working in batches if necessary, arrange the baguette slices in the pan in a single layer and grill until they are lightly toasted and you see grill marks, 1 to 2 minutes on each side. Set the crostini aside to cool.

3. Heat the oil in a large skillet over medium heat. Add the mushrooms and sauté until tender and browned, 5 to 7 minutes. Stir in the garlic and salt and cook until the garlic is fragrant and tender, 3 to 5 minutes more. Stir in the Marsala, rosemary, and thyme and cook until the wine has been absorbed by the mushrooms, 3 to 5 minutes.

4. Add the truffle oil to the mushrooms, stir, and then add the grated Parmesan and the Gruyère. Stir the mixture until the cheeses have melted. Transfer the mixture to a food processor and process until almost smooth. Set aside.

5. Heat a small skillet over medium-low heat. Add the bacon and cook until crisp, turning once, about 5 minutes. Transfer the bacon to paper towels to drain. When it is cool, chop it into small pieces.

6. To assemble the crostini, spread 1 tablespoon of the mushroom pâté on each grilled crostini. Decorate each with 4 to 5 cornichon slices and several Parmesan shavings, and dot with a few bacon bits. Serve warm, at room temp or cold.

Keep It Simple

- To make your shopping list shorter, use just one type of mushroom, all Parmesan for your cheese, and either thyme or rosemary, not both.
- Marsala wine has a distinctive musty, dry flavor, but you could try sherry or red wine as a substitution. Or to go alcohol-free, you can substitute 1 tablespoon of Worcestershire sauce.
- Truffle oil is a luxury ingredient; the flavor is deeply mushroom and simply intoxicating. You can also get this flavor through truffle butter instead of oil. Both are a little pricey, but you only use a touch per recipe.

50/50

If your diners are not into meat, omit the bacon from some or all of the crostini. And if desired, add a sprinkle of coarse sea salt or smoked sea salt instead, to mimic the salty bite of the bacon.

Spicy Green Pepper + Edamame Crostini

MAKES 15 CROSTINI

10-in-20

Colorful vegetables get all the love. Red, orange, and yellow veggies are always grabbing our attention at the grocery store, screaming at us to buy them. Sometimes I don't want a supersweet red or yellow pepper, sometimes I WANT the pepper to have a bit of a bite. And green peppers have just that, along with a lighter, fresher flavor. Plus they are often less than half the price of red peppers. So let's make them the star this time around; let's make them spicy and smoky, and create a crostini that celebrates being green. Red peppers need not apply.

1 baguette, cut into fifteen ¼-inch-thick slices

1 cup shelled edamame (fresh or frozen)

Finely grated zest and juice of 1 lime

3 tablespoons extra-virgin olive oil

1 teaspoon kosher salt

1 large green bell pepper, cored, seeded, and finely chopped

1 scallion, thinly sliced

½ jalapeño chile, seeds and ribs removed, finely chopped

1 garlic clove, minced

¼ teaspoon smoked paprika

⅓ cup crumbled or finely chopped feta cheese (2 ounces)

1. Preheat a grill pan over high heat. Working in batches if necessary, arrange the baguette slices in it in a single layer and cook until they are lightly toasted and you see grill marks 1 to 2 minutes on each side. Set the crostini aside to cool.

2. Put the edamame, lime juice, lime zest, 2 tablespoons of the oil, and ½ teaspoon of the salt in a food processor. Process until pureed.

3. Heat the remaining 1 tablespoon oil in a small skillet over medium heat. Stir in the green peppers, scallion, jalapeño, garlic, the remaining ½ teaspoon salt, and the paprika. Cook, stirring occasionally, until the bell peppers are tender but not mushy, 5 to 7 minutes; you want them just firm enough to have a slight bite.

4. To assemble, spread 1 tablespoon of the edamame mixture on each crostini and then cover with 1 tablespoon of the pepper mixture. Arrange the crostini on a serving plate, and scatter 1 teaspoon of the cheese on top of each.

Keep It Simple

• Though I really prefer green peppers in this recipe, red, yellow, or orange also work if that's what you have on hand.

• Edamame are soybeans and they pack a lot of great fiber and protein along with their vibrant green color, but they can be replaced with cannellini beans, black beans, or chickpeas.

• Feel free to substitute a pinch of crushed red pepper flakes or ground cayenne for the jalapeño if you prefer.

Zucchini Crostini with Pomegranate–Goat Cheese Spread

MAKES 15 CROSTINI

10-in-20

Mild, tender-crisp zucchini is the perfect vehicle for a terrific goat cheese spread, a gluten-free wonder just waiting to be topped and devoured. So now you can have fun saying, and eating, your zucchini crostini!

4 ounces cream cheese, at room temperature

2 ounces soft goat cheese, at room temperature

2 teaspoons minced fresh thyme leaves

Finely grated zest of ½ lemon

½ teaspoon kosher salt

¼ cup dried cranberries

1 large zucchini, cut diagonally into fifteen ¼-inch-thick slices

¼ cup pomegranate seeds (see Appendix, page 261)

1. Blend the cream cheese, goat cheese, thyme, lemon zest, and ¼ teaspoon of the salt in a medium bowl. Stir in the cranberries, distributing them evenly.

2. Sprinkle the remaining ¼ teaspoon salt over both sides of the zucchini slices and arrange the slices on a serving platter. Divide the cheese mixture smoothly over the slices and top each with a generous sprinkling of the pomegranate seeds and extra lemon zest if desired.

Keep It Simple

• This pomegranate goat cheese combo is one of my all-time favorite spreads and it works great on classic crackers or bread, too. Just be sure to fold the pomegranate seeds into the spread if you use it this way.

• While I'm crazy for the goat cheese, these zucchini crostini are super versatile and can be topped with everything from Beet Hummus (page 37) to crab salad (use the Crab-Stuffed Endive recipe, page 46, omitting the frisée and endive).

• All you can find are small zucchini? Not a problem. Just cut the zucchini on more of a diagonal for larger slices.

Buffalo Cabbage Spring Rolls

MAKES 6 SPRING ROLLS; ABOUT 1 CUP DIPPING SAUCE

FF | 50/50

Growing up in Buffalo isn't exactly glamorous, but the best part about living there is that there are always plenty of wings to go around. But a plate of wings is more "Meat in the Middle" than "Meat on the Side," so I decided to twist this Buffalonian classic. I kept some chicken, added lots of crunchy cabbage, threw in some fresh celery, and smothered it all in an addictingly spicy and creamy Buffalo sauce. So, imagine yourself in Buffalo, cozy on the couch, watching the snow fall outside even though it's only September, and noshing on these perfectly crispy Buffalo Cabbage Spring Rolls with your best friend Andy by your side. Kind of makes you want to move to Buffalo, doesn't it?

Blue Cheese Dipping Sauce

½ cup blue cheese crumbles (2 ounces)

¼ cup sour cream

2 tablespoons buttermilk

3 tablespoons finely chopped scallions, green parts only

¼ teaspoon kosher salt

Buffalo Cabbage Spring Rolls

1 teaspoon extra-virgin olive oil

1 boneless, skinless chicken breast half (6 ounces)

1 teaspoon kosher salt

½ teaspoon ground black pepper

3 ounces cream cheese

⅓ cup Frank's RedHot Original Cayenne Pepper Sauce

2½ cups lightly packed cabbage slaw mix (from the supermarket)

¾ cup finely chopped celery

¼ cup finely chopped scallions

¼ cup coarsely chopped fresh cilantro

½ teaspoon garlic powder

6 flour egg roll wrappers

Canola oil, for frying

Blue Cheese Dipping Sauce

Put the blue cheese crumbles in a small bowl, breaking up the pieces if they are larger than ¼ inch. Add the sour cream, buttermilk, scallions, and salt to the bowl and stir to combine. Set aside.

Buffalo Cabbage Spring Rolls

1. Heat the oil in a small skillet over medium heat. Sprinkle ½ teaspoon of the salt and ¼ teaspoon of the pepper evenly all over the chicken. Add the chicken to the skillet and cook until golden brown on both sides and cooked through, about 6 minutes per side. Transfer the chicken to a cutting board to rest for 2 to 3 minutes; then chop it into ½-inch pieces.

2. Put the cream cheese and hot sauce in a large microwave-safe bowl and microwave on high until the cheese has softened slightly, 15 to 20 seconds. Whisk the mixture until well combined. It does not have to be perfectly smooth; it's okay to have some lumps. Add the chicken, slaw mix, celery, scallions, cilantro, garlic powder, the remaining ½ teaspoon salt, and ¼ teaspoon pepper to the bowl and stir until well combined.

3. Arrange the egg roll wrappers on a work surface, orienting each so one corner points toward you (making a diamond shape). Have ready a small bowl of water and a pastry brush. Make the rolls one at a time: Spoon about ½ cup of the filling onto the center and then brush a little water onto the margins. Fold up the bottom corner over the filling; then fold up each side corner. Then roll the filled wrapper over on itself toward the top corner.

4. Pour oil into a small or medium heavy-bottomed saucepan to a depth of at least 2 inches but not more than halfway up the sides. Place the pan over medium-high heat and bring the oil to 375°F; use a candy thermometer to register the temperature. Working in small batches, fry the rolls until they are golden brown on all sides, 4 to 6 minutes. Transfer each batch to a paper towel–lined plate to drain.

5. Serve the rolls hot with Blue Cheese Dipping Sauce.

Keep It Simple

- I don't always have buttermilk on hand, and although it adds a little extra tang to the dipping sauce, it can easily be replaced with any milk or cream you have in your fridge.
- Take a shortcut from the store and buy a precooked rotisserie chicken instead of cooking the breast yourself.

FF

Kids aren't big fans of blue cheese? Leave it out for a scallion–sour cream dressing. To tone down the spicy taste, cut the amount of hot sauce to 3 tablespoons and use 5 ounces of cream cheese instead for a milder version.

50/50

There are many times I choose to serve meatless. To make half the recipe meatless, use only 3 ounces chicken, but add an extra ½ cup slaw mix; (don't add the chicken to the filling until after you've made 3 vegetarian rolls. Or to go totally meat-free, simply replace all the chicken with an extra cup of the slaw mix.

Pesto + Balsamic Tomato Bombs

MAKES 15 STUFFED CHERRY TOMATOES

10-in-20

These tomato bombs are so good, so simple, and SO cute. But these little guys and I didn't always have the strong, loving relationship we have today. I have to take the blame on this one. See, I had decided that they were the perfect thing to serve at a big event I was doing. By tomato number 562, I was cursing the day I ever came up with this amazing appetizer. So please, don't try and make 1,800 of them, but do make 15, 30, or even 45.

2 tablespoons balsamic vinegar

15 cherry tomatoes

2 ounces cream cheese, at room temperature

2 teaspoons Basil Pesto (see page 163)

1 Persian cucumber, cut into fifteen rounds

Toothpicks

1. Heat the vinegar in a very small skillet or saucepan over medium heat and cook until it is thick and syrupy, 5 to 7 minutes. Once reduced, there should be 1 to 1½ teaspoons remaining in the skillet.

2. Blend the cream cheese and pesto in a small bowl and then stir in the vinegar until well combined.

3. Cut off the bottom third of each tomato (the end with no stem) and set it aside. Using a melon baller or paring knife, hollow out the larger, two-thirds section of each tomato. Fill the tomatoes with the cream cheese mixture, top each with a cucumber slice followed by the cut-off bottom section. Poke a toothpick through each to hold the layers together and serve.

Keep It Simple

If your store doesn't carry Persian cucumbers you can leave them off or slice a regular cucumber into rounds and then cut the rounds into quarters. They should be the perfect size.

Broccoli + Lamb Samosas

MAKES 15 SAMOSAS

50/50 | 500↓

They say that a few key accessories can make an outfit; well, the same is true for your food. Have a couple key seasonings on hand like ginger and curry powder and you can create exotic and interesting flavors. In these samosas a little fresh ginger, curry powder, and peanut butter create a savory filling that dances around on your tongue and is sure to impress your guests. And don't worry, the ginger will last months in your freezer and the curry powder stays vibrant in your cabinet, so you will always have them on hand as you learn to weave them into all your favorite meals.

2 tablespoons olive oil, plus more as needed

½ pound ground lamb

3 cups very finely chopped broccoli (1½ pounds)

2 garlic cloves, minced

1½ teaspoons kosher salt

1 teaspoon peeled and grated fresh ginger

1 cup shelled edamame (fresh or frozen)

½ cup water

¼ cup peanut butter

1 teaspoon curry powder

Finely grated zest and juice of 1 lime

4 tablespoons (½ stick) unsalted butter

Eight 14 × 18-inch sheets phyllo dough

¾ cup sour cream

2 tablespoons chopped fresh mint leaves

1. Heat the oil in a large skillet over medium-high heat. Add the lamb and cook, stirring with a wooden spoon to break up, until browned and cooked through, 5 to 8 minutes. Using a slotted spoon, transfer the lamb to a large bowl.

2. Return the skillet to the heat and add more oil if it is dry. Stir in the broccoli, garlic, salt, and ginger and cook until the broccoli is tender, about 5 minutes. Return the lamb to the skillet and stir in the edamame, water, peanut butter, curry powder, and lime zest. Continue to cook, stirring, until the peanut butter has melted and the edamame has thawed (if you started with frozen), about 2 minutes.

3. Spoon the broccoli mixture back into the large bowl and refrigerate for at least 10 minutes; the filling can be warm, but not hot, when you fill the samosas.

4. Preheat the oven to 375°F. Cut the phyllo sheets into 30 strips, each about 3 × 18-inches using a pizza cutter or chefs knife; don't worry about getting the width perfect! Keep the phyllo pieces covered with a lightly dampened towel while you work; otherwise they will dry out and break. In a small microwave-safe bowl, microwave the butter on high for 30 seconds until melted. Lay a strip of phyllo on a work surface, oriented with one 3-inch end toward you. Using a pastry brush, brush a little melted butter over the phyllo and then lay a second strip on top of the first. Place ¼ cup of the filling on the phyllo near the lower left edge and, leaving the lower right corner bare; then fold the lower right corner up over the filling so that the lower right corner is now touching the left edge and you have formed a triangle. Then fold the triangle up and over to itself; continue to fold back and forth up the entire length of the phyllo. Repeat the layering, filling, and folding with the rest of phyllo and filling. (Go to NikkiDinkiCooking.com for step-by-step photos.)

5. Arrange the samosas on a baking sheet, brush the tops with the melted butter, and place in the oven to bake until golden brown, 20 to 25 minutes. While they bake, whisk together the sour cream and lime juice in a small bowl, then stir in the mint. Serve the samosas hot with the mint dipping sauce.

Keep It Simple

- Phyllo dough comes in many different size sheets. If you can't find 14 × 18, do a little math and just buy enough to cut into thirty 3 × 18-inch strips (a little shorter works, too). And any brand should have enough sheets to make double this recipe.
- You could use pie dough instead of phyllo, or even stuff the filling in a pita.
- You want the pieces of broccoli to be very small, so save time by chopping your broccoli in the food processor: 10 pulses should work just fine.
- As I mentioned above, fresh ginger should be stored in your freezer, wrapped in plastic wrap. When you want to use it simply grate it frozen.
- My husband loves lamb and it works great here, but it can be replaced with ground chicken, beef, or turkey for an equally flavorful bite.

50/50

To make this dish vegetarian, omit the lamb and use 1 more cup broccoli and ½ cup more edamame.

Salads

Red + Green Salad
with Apricot Dressing + Pork Croutons

MAKES 2 LARGE OR 4 SMALL SERVINGS, WITH ABOUT ¾ CUP APRICOT DRESSING

500↓ | FF | 50/50

My sister Gina lives near me. Sometimes we meet at a neighborhood spot for the early bird special. One of my favorite dishes is a salad that has a tangy, sweet dressing. But while the idea is there, this dish could be better. My improved version puts pieces of panfried, crunchy pork croûtons that you won't soon forget on top of cool, crunchy greens with apricots and tomatoes all wrapped up in a dressing that you will want to put on everything. So enjoy, and take a minute to catch up with your sister and tell her things such as, if she leaves New York City you will never speak to her again . . . . :)

Apricot Dressing

½ cup apricot or peach jam

3 tablespoons white wine vinegar

1 teaspoon Dijon mustard

Finely grated zest of ½ lime

½ teaspoon kosher salt

⅛ teaspoon ground black pepper

Pork Croutons

¼ cup all-purpose flour

¼ teaspoon kosher salt

¼ teaspoon ground black pepper

1 large egg

1 tablespoon water

3 tablespoons olive oil

½ pound boneless pork chop, cut into bite-size pieces

¾ cup seasoned dry bread crumbs

Red + Green Salad

1 small head red leaf lettuce, coarsely chopped

1 small head green leaf lettuce, coarsely chopped

2 medium beefsteak tomatoes, cut into bite-size wedges

½ red onion, thinly sliced

3 apricots or peaches, pitted and cut into bite-size pieces

Apricot Dressing

Whisk together the jam, vinegar, mustard, lime zest, salt, and pepper in a small bowl, mixing until well combined. Set aside.

Pork Croutons

1. Whisk together the flour, ⅛ teaspoon of the salt, and ⅛ teaspoon of the pepper in a shallow bowl. Whisk together the egg, water, the remaining ⅛ teaspoon salt, and the remaining ⅛ teaspoon pepper in a second shallow bowl. Put the bread crumbs in a third shallow bowl. (If you haven't got your salad ingredients cut up, do so now!)

2. Heat the oil in a large skillet over medium heat. While it's heating, toss the pork in the flour and then lift out the pieces, shaking off the excess flour. Transfer them to the egg mixture and stir to coat with the egg. Lift out the pieces, letting the excess egg drip off, then transfer them to the bread crumbs. Stir to make sure all sides are coated with crumbs.

3. Transfer the pork to the skillet and cook until crispy brown on all sides and cooked through, about 5 minutes. Transfer the croutons to paper towels to drain.

Red + Green Salad

1. Put the red lettuce, green lettuce, tomatoes, apricots, and onion in a large bowl and gently toss to mix.

2. Add half the dressing to the salad and gently toss until combined. Add more dressing as desired. Divide the salad among four small or two large plates and top each serving with the warm croutons.

FF

With the sweet dressing, mild lettuce, and yummy pork, your whole family will be asking for seconds. But if you have some extra-picky eaters, try omitting the red onion and chopping the tomatoes and fruit extra small.

50/50

Without the pork, this salad is still great, but it's a little light to have as your main meal. If you're looking for something more satisfying, cube and pat dry some extra-firm tofu, run the tofu through the same breading process, and fry just like the pork. Or use my eggplant croutons (see page 72) for a very veggie crouton.

Kale Caesar Salad + Eggplant Croutons

MAKES 4 SERVINGS; ABOUT 1¼ CUPS CAESAR DRESSING

FF | 50/50

I've always been a Caesar salad fan. By adding this classic dressing to kale instead of the usual romaine lettuce you have a more nutritious version that has great texture and bite. Top with some shaved Parmesan for a hit of cheesy richness, pomegranate seeds for some acidic punch, and of course eggplant croutons, and this is a Caesar salad fit for a king. In case you missed it, I said EGGPLANT CROUTONS: crunchy, bready, warm bites where the eggplant almost melts away. If you can't tell already, I think it's kind of awesome!

Caesar Dressing

¾ cup grated Parmesan cheese (3 ounces)

½ cup mayonnaise

½ cup Greek yogurt

Juice of ½ lemon

2 teaspoons Worcestershire sauce

2 teaspoons anchovy paste

1 teaspoon Dijon mustard

1 small garlic clove, minced

¼ teaspoon cayenne pepper, plus more to taste

Eggplant Croutons

⅓ cup all-purpose flour

½ teaspoon kosher salt

2 large eggs

2 teaspoons water

1 cup Italian-style bread crumbs

2 tablespoons olive oil

1 small eggplant, peeled and cut into ½-inch cubes

Kale Salad

One 1-pound bunch kale

4 chicken cutlets (2 to 3 ounces each)

½ teaspoon kosher salt

¼ teaspoon paprika

⅛ teaspoon ground black pepper

½ cup pomegranate seeds (see Appendix, page 261)

¼ cup shaved Parmesan cheese

Caesar Dressing

Put the Parmesan, mayonnaise, yogurt, lemon juice, Worcestershire sauce, anchovy paste, mustard, garlic, and cayenne in a food processor. Process until combined and smooth. The dressing should have some kick, so taste and add more cayenne if necessary. Set aside.

Eggplant Croutons

1. Whisk together the flour and salt in a shallow bowl. Whisk together the egg and water in a second shallow bowl. Put the bread crumbs in a third shallow bowl.

2. Heat the oil in a large skillet over medium heat. While it's heating, toss the eggplant in the flour and lift out the pieces, shaking off the excess flour. Transfer them to the egg mixture and stir them to coat with the egg. Lift out the pieces, letting the excess egg drip off, then transfer them to the bread crumbs; stir to make sure all sides are coated with crumbs.

3. Preheat the oven to 220°F. Transfer the eggplant pieces to the skillet and cook until crispy brown on all sides, 5 to 7 minutes. Transfer the croutons to a paper towel–lined plate to drain, then place in the oven to keep warm while you make the salad.

Kale Salad

1. Stem the kale and chop or cut the leaves into ¼- to ½-inch-wide strips; you should have about 10 cups of lightly packed kale. Put the kale in a large bowl. Add the dressing and toss until combined. Set aside.

2. Preheat a large skillet over medium-high heat. While it's heating, sprinkle the chicken on all sides with the salt, paprika, and pepper. Arrange the chicken in the skillet in a single layer and cook until lightly browned on both sides and cooked through, 2 to 3 minutes per side. Transfer to a cutting board to rest for 2 minutes then cut each cutlet into ½-inch-wide strips.

3. To serve, divide the kale among four bowls or plates. Top each serving with 1 cutlet, one-quarter of the croutons, 2 tablespoons of the pomegranate seeds, and 1 tablespoon of the Parmesan shavings.

FF

- Switch out the kale for classic romaine, baby spinach, or iceberg lettuce.
- No matter what, definitely leave the eggplant croutons on this dish; the texture of the eggplant changes when cooked and your kids will just think it's a regular crouton.

50/50

Without the meat, this dish serves more as a side dish or light lunch. For something more substantial but still meat-free, add chickpeas, extra eggplant croutons, and/or a fried egg—perfection.

Kale Caesar Salad
+ Eggplant Croutons (p. 71)

Escarole Salad with
Pesto Dressing +
Chickpea Crunchies (p. 74)

Escarole Salad
with Pesto Dressing + Chickpea Crunchies

MAKES 2 LARGE OR 4 SMALL SERVINGS

500↓

When I have dinner parties I like to get a list of what my friends like to eat so I can include some of their favorite things. The bottom line is if some of their most loved flavors are in the meal, they are going to have a better experience. So when I saw pesto topping our friend Phil's list, I knew I wanted to incorporate it into my dinner but to do something different with it. I came up with this salad, which has the strong flavor of the pesto with the tang of vinegar and the creaminess of Greek yogurt, draped over soft escarole. Top with baked spiced chickpeas and enjoy!

1 head escarole

One 15-ounce can chickpeas, rinsed and drained

2 teaspoons olive oil

1 teaspoon Creole seasoning or your favorite blend

1 teaspoon kosher salt

¼ cup Basil Pesto (see page 163)

½ cup Greek yogurt

3 tablespoons white wine vinegar

½ cup dried cranberries

1. Preheat the oven to 400°F. Coarsely chop or tear the escarole leaves and set aside in a large bowl. Toss the chickpeas with the oil, Creole seasoning, and ½ teaspoon of the salt (leave the salt off if there is already salt in your Creole seasoning) in a medium bowl. Spread the chickpeas out on a rimmed baking sheet and bake until pleasingly crunchy, 25 to 40 minutes (taste after 25 minutes; bake longer if you want them crunchier).

2. While the chickpeas bake, make the dressing: Whisk together the pesto, Greek yogurt, vinegar, and remaining ½ teaspoon salt in a small bowl.

3. To serve, add the dressing to the escarole and toss to coat. Divide the escarole among four small or two large bowls and then divide the chickpea crunchies and cranberries evenly atop each.

Butternut Squash Wedge Salad
with Buttermilk–Blue Cheese Dressing

MAKES 4 SERVINGS; ABOUT 2 CUPS DRESSING

500↓ | FF | 50/50

It's true, you might not see smoky and sweet butternut squash as a regular topping choice for your salad at the corner deli, but that's because the deli crew are simply falling behind the times. Butternut squash with the addition of smoked paprika and cayenne makes the perfect topping for a super-crunchy wedge salad. The squash gives a depth of flavor and baconlike taste to the otherwise tangy dressing and elevates this salad to the next level. Come on, let's be trendsetters, let's put squash on our salads! I guarantee you, before you know it, everyone will be doing it!

Buttermilk–Blue Cheese Dressing

½ cup mayonnaise

4 scallions, cut into 2-inch lengths

¼ cup fresh flat-leaf parsley leaves

2 garlic cloves

¾ cup Greek yogurt

¼ cup buttermilk

Juice of 1 lemon

1 teaspoon Dijon mustard

1 teaspoon kosher salt

¼ teaspoon ground black pepper

½ cup blue cheese crumbles

Butternut Squash Wedge Salad

One 1-pound butternut squash

2 bacon strips

1 tablespoon olive oil

1 teaspoon kosher salt

¼ teaspoon smoked paprika

¼ teaspoon cayenne pepper

1 medium head iceberg lettuce, cut to 4 wedges

2 radishes, thinly sliced

Buttermilk–Blue Cheese Dressing

Put the mayonnaise, scallions, parsley, garlic, yogurt, buttermilk, lemon juice, mustard, salt, and pepper in a food processor and process until the mixture is smooth and the herbs are finely chopped. Scrape the dressing into a small bowl and fold in the cheese crumbles. Set aside.

Butternut Squash Wedge Salad

1. Preheat the oven to 400°F.

2. Peel the squash. Cut it in half lengthwise and, using a soupspoon, scoop out the seeds. Chop the flesh into ¼-inch pieces. Clean any fibers from the seeds and spread out the seeds on a rimmed baking sheet. Set aside.

3. Lay the bacon on a second baking sheet lined with foil and bake in the oven until crisp, 15 to 20 minutes. Transfer the bacon to a paper towel and place the baking sheet with the squash seeds in the oven. Roast the seeds until they are crisp and slightly browned, 5 to 7 minutes. Meanwhile, chop the bacon on a cutting board into small pieces.

4. Heat the oil in a large skillet over medium-high heat. Stir in the chopped squash, salt, paprika, and cayenne. Sauté until the squash is tender and browned on all sides, 10 to 12 minutes.

5. To serve, place a lettuce wedge on each of four plates. Ladle ¼ cup of the dressing over each wedge. Divide the radishes, sautéed squash, squash seeds, and chopped bacon equally among the servings, letting them spill over the lettuce onto the plate. Pass the extra dressing at the table.

Keep It Simple

- You can use regular paprika instead of smoked if that's all you have on hand. Or half regular paprika and half chili powder; ancho chili powder is nice and mimics the smoky flavor of smoked paprika.
- If any dressing remains at the end of the meal, cover it and refrigerate for up to 3 days.

FF

By making your own dressing you are saving your family from the load of sugar that is normally found in the store-bought brands. And if your family doesn't love blue cheese, you can replace it with goat cheese or feta for a fun, tangy twist that's milder.

50/50

Simply omit the bacon from any portions you want to be vegetarian; the spiced squash has a similar warm and smoky taste and the bacon will not be missed. You can add the extra to the other servings, no one will complain!

Grilled Romaine + Radicchio Salad

MAKES 4 SERVINGS; ABOUT 1 CUP DRESSING

500↓ | Make It Meaty

I LOVE this salad. Yes, LOVE. The char from the grill, the slightly bitter radicchio sweetened up by a dressing of honey and orange, and then the burst of fresh grapes to brighten up the smokiness. Make this for your next dinner party, make it tonight, heck make it for breakfast—just make it!

Honey-Orange Dressing

½ cup Greek yogurt

¼ cup mayonnaise

¼ cup orange juice

1 tablespoon honey

1 teaspoon white wine vinegar

½ teaspoon kosher salt

1 teaspoon finely chopped fresh chives

Romaine + Radicchio Salad

2 romaine lettuce hearts, cut lengthwise into 8 wedges

1 radicchio, cut lengthwise into 4 wedges

1 red onion, cut lengthwise into 8 wedges

2 tablespoons olive oil

1 teaspoon kosher salt

1½ cups halved red grapes

Honey-Orange Dressing

Add the yogurt, mayonnaise, orange juice, honey, vinegar, and salt to a medium bowl. Whisk together until well blended; then whisk in the chives.

Romaine + Radicchio Salad

1. Preheat a gas or charcoal grill (or preheat a grill pan). Brush the oil over all surfaces of the romaine, radicchio, and onion wedges, then sprinkle evenly with the salt. Arrange the romaine, radicchio, and onion wedges on the hot grill or grill pan. Cook until all pieces are slightly wilted and charred on all cut sides (leave the uncut sides raw), 1 to 2 minutes per side for the romaine and radicchio; 2 to 4 minutes per side for the onions.

2. To serve, divide the romaine, radicchio, and onion wedges among four plates. Ladle one-quarter of the dressing over each serving. Divide the grapes equally and scatter over the tops.

Tarragon + Golden Raisin Coleslaw

MAKES ABOUT 6 CUPS COLESLAW

10-in-20 | 500↓ | FF

Here is a coleslaw with enough twists and turns to keep even a refined palate interested while still being as satisfying as the familiar classic. Some licorice-y tarragon, sweet golden raisins, and sumac all make it special enough for a dinner party yet absolutely perfect for a backyard barbecue.

4 cups shredded cabbage or purchased
    coleslaw mix

1 cup thinly sliced celery

½ Granny Smith apple, cored and julienned

1 cup golden raisins

6 tablespoons champagne vinegar

¼ cup mayonnaise

1 tablespoon kosher salt

1 tablespoon ground sumac

2 teaspoons finely chopped fresh tarragon leaves

1. Put the cabbage, celery, apples, and raisins in a large bowl and mix well using your hands.

2. To make the dressing, whisk together the vinegar, mayonnaise, salt, and sumac in a small bowl until well combined. Whisk in the tarragon.

3. To complete the coleslaw, stir the dressing into the cabbage mixture, tossing gently until well combined. You can serve the slaw immediately or refrigerate it, covered, for up to 3 days.

Keep It Simple

Sumac has a tart berry flavor; you can use 1½ teaspoons paprika and the finely grated zest of 1 lemon instead, or simply leave it out. The salad really pops with the sumac, and is just a little different, but it is still great without it.

FF

• If you want to replace it, parsley and basil are great options instead.

• This slaw only gets better as it sits, so let it sit in your fridge all day or even overnight before serving.

Tarragon + Golden Raisin
Coleslaw

Cauliflower, Lentils
+ Orange Salad (p. 82)

Cauliflower, Lentils + Orange Salad

MAKES 4 SERVINGS

500↓ | Make It Meaty

My husband is not a picky man. He is still counting his blessings that the girl who ate almost nothing and cooked even less has somehow turned into a chef with a flair for veggies. He is totally happy to let me determine the contents of our fridge, with one exception: There must be orange juice on hand at all times. He considers it the most perfect beverage and thinks it pairs well with everything from steak to pasta. So, when cooking up a warm salad of lentils (a favorite of his) and cauliflower (a second favorite), I had him on my mind and thought "why not work some OJ into the dressing?" The result is uniquely orangey and totally addictive.

Cauliflower, Lentils + Orange Salad

1 medium head cauliflower

1 tablespoon olive oil

2 teaspoons kosher salt

1¼ cups green or brown lentils

2½ cups water

1 orange, peeled, segments separated and cut to
    1-inch chunks

1 medium cucumber, finely chopped

1 small orange bell pepper, cored, seeded,
    and finely chopped

2 tablespoons chopped fresh mint leaves

¾ cup finely chopped scallions,
    plus more for garnish

Orange Dressing

¼ cup orange juice

2 tablespoons white wine vinegar

1 tablespoon agave nectar

1 teaspoon Dijon mustard

1 teaspoon kosher salt

¼ teaspoon ground black pepper

1 garlic clove, grated

¼ cup extra-virgin olive oil

Cauliflower, Lentils + Orange Salad

1. Preheat the oven to 450°F. Cut the cauliflower into medium florets and spread them out on a rimmed baking sheet. Drizzle with the oil and sprinkle with 1 teaspoon of the salt. Roast in the oven until tender and brown, 30 to 35 minutes, stirring halfway through.

$2.$ Meanwhile, put the lentils and water into a medium saucepan and bring to a boil. Reduce the heat to medium, cover, and cook until the lentils are tender but al dente, about 20 minutes or as indicated on the package directions. If there is still water in the pan when the lentils are done, simply drain it. While the lentils cook, make the Orange Dressing (below).

$3.$ Put the cauliflower and lentils in a large bowl. Add the oranges, bell pepper, cucumbers, mint, scallions, the remaining 1 teaspoon salt, and the dressing and stir to mix well. Serve the salad warm or at room temperature with some additional scallions scattered over the top.

Orange Dressing

Whisk together the orange juice, vinegar, agave nectar, mustard, salt, pepper, and garlic in a small bowl. Slowly whisk in the oil until well combined.

Keep It Simple

- To get this dinner to the table superfast, start with cooked lentils from your grocery store and sauté the cauliflower for 7 to 10 minutes instead of roasting it.
- If you don't have OJ on hand like I do, buy 2 oranges instead of 1 for this recipe; use 1 for the segments and the other for the juice for the dressing.
- Chop the cucumber and bell pepper into small (¼-inch) pieces so the raw pieces give lots of bright little bursts of flavor.
- I always have fresh herbs either growing in my garden or stuffed in my fridge, so I like to use mint as well as scallions in this recipe. If you don't have herbs readily available, or want to save a buck, stick just to scallions.

Make It Meaty

Bump up the protein in this dish by adding cooked, cubed pork, chicken, or shrimp. Also, chickpeas and black beans are great nonmeat add-ins that pack a protein punch.

Fennel-Orange Caprese
with Spicy Balsamic Drizzle

MAKES 4 SERVINGS

10-in-20 | 500↓

My friend Damaris has an incredible show on Food Network called *Southern at Heart*. Recently I traveled to Kentucky to join her on an episode where she served up a stewed tomato caprese salad with lemon. Damaris's take on a caprese was perfectly her, classic and comforting but with the volume turned up. When I returned I set out to make my version. I started out by reducing balsamic vinegar until it is thick, syrupy, and sweet. I added heat and tartness, poured it over juicy oranges and creamy fresh mozzarella that are sitting on a bed of shaved fennel, and you have my fresh and bright version of the classic.

¾ cup balsamic vinegar

½ teaspoon cayenne pepper

½ teaspoon ground sumac

3 oranges

½ fennel bulb, very thinly sliced

¼ teaspoon kosher salt

1 pound fresh mozzarella, cut into ½-inch-thick slices

1 tablespoon extra-virgin olive oil

¼ cup chopped fresh mint leaves

1. Add the vinegar, cayenne, and sumac to a small saucepan, place over medium heat, and whisk together briefly. Cook until the vinegar is thick and syrupy, about 8 minutes. Keep an eye on the reduction as it can burn easily; reduce the heat if necessary, and bear in mind it will thicken more as it cools.

2. Meanwhile, using a sharp knife, cut away the peel and pith from the oranges. Then cut the middle portion of each orange crosswise into ½-inch-thick rounds leaving the ends. Squeeze the juice from the ends of the oranges into a medium bowl. Add the fennel and salt and gently toss to combine.

3. To serve, lift the fennel from the juice and arrange it in a single layer along the center of a platter. Divide the orange slices and mozzarella over the fennel, overlapping them in alternating sequence. Drizzle first the oil and then some of the balsamic syrup over the top and then sprinkle with the mint.

Caponata Panzanella

MAKES 6 SMALL OR 4 LARGE SERVINGS

500↓ | Make It Meaty

My father in-law, Bob, was the first to introduce me to caponata. The flavors marry and transform into something that is truly a treat. It's tart and sweet with a unique flavor all its own. The only way that you can make it better is to add chunks of crusty bread and create a caponata panzanella. Then all the flavors you love in a caponata are being soaked up by the bread. And with the whole thing studded with mini mozzarella balls it is SO good. Let me repeat, SO GOOD!

1 medium eggplant (¾ pound)

2 tablespoons olive oil

2½ teaspoons kosher salt

1 ciabatta loaf

1 medium red onion, thinly sliced

2 celery ribs, cut crosswise into ¼-inch-thick slices

1 small fennel bulb, thinly sliced, with a few fronds reserved for garnish

1 orange bell pepper, cored, seeded, and cut into ½-inch pieces

3 garlic cloves, minced

2 tablespoons tomato paste

¼ cup red wine vinegar

¼ cup golden raisins

2 tablespoons capers, drained

2 tablespoons pine nuts

1 tablespoon sugar

8 ounces fresh mozzarella mini balls (or a chunk cut into ½-inch cubes)

1 small cucumber, very thinly sliced

1. Preheat the oven to 400°F.

2. Using a paring knife, peel the eggplant, removing about half the skin in strips to create a striped effect. Cut the eggplant into 1-inch cubes. Toss them in a large bowl with 1 tablespoon of the oil and 1 teaspoon of the salt; then spread them out on a rimmed baking sheet. Bake the eggplant until it is slightly browned and soft but not mushy, 15 to 20 minutes. Set aside.

3. Meanwhile, cut the ciabatta into 1-inch cubes. Spread the cubes out on a second rimmed baking sheet and bake until very lightly toasted, 3 to 5 minutes. You don't want them brown but rather a little crispy and a little dried out. Set aside.

4. Heat the remaining 1 tablespoon oil in a large skillet over medium-high heat. Stir in the onion, celery, fennel, pepper, garlic, and the remaining 1½ teaspoons salt and sauté until the vegetables are tender but still slightly crisp, about 7 minutes.

5. Add the tomato paste to the skillet and stir until dissolved; cook for 2 minutes. Stir in the eggplant, vinegar, raisins, capers, pine nuts, and sugar and cook until the vinegar is absorbed and the sugar has dissolved, about 3 minutes.

6. Transfer the hot eggplant mixture to a large serving bowl, immediately add the ciabatta cubes, and toss to mix. Let the salad cool slightly; then mix in the mozzarella and cucumbers. Top with the fennel fronds, serve, and enjoy!

Keep It Simple

Panzanella is a salad traditionally made with day-old bread and tomatoes. You can use bread that is a little stale and then there is no need to dry it out in step 3. You can also use any bread you like; I find that bread with a crisper crust works best. An Italian loaf, French baguette, or artisan sourdough would all work great.

Make It Meaty

I like to serve hot Tiny Chicken Meatballs (page 223) over the top of this panzanella. The mix is satisfying and full of flavor.

Winter Greens

We all know that we should eat our greens; the darker the green the better they are for you with Vitamins A, C, E, folate, iron, and calcium! Really, greens are the original superfood, but many of them can be bitter and tough, making them a little hard to love. So what I like to do is take those greens and add them to pot pies, incorporate them in crepe batter, form them into little shells to bake eggs in, and use their texture and hues to add interest to salads. My goal is to get you to love every vegetable, and that means my dishes HAVE to be yummy. Sure, these dishes are packed with green goodness, but first and foremost they are simply delicious!

Recipe List

Broccoli

Amazingly this mini green tree is for the most part popular, enjoyed by everyone, both young and old. And it should be! In just one cup of cooked broccoli you're getting double and triple the amount of Vitamin K and C you need in a day, along with 50 percent of your daily recommended amount of folate and about 20 percent of your daily recommended amount of fiber. All that and more for just a measly 55 calories, which means you are definitely having dessert tonight. But if you are so over steamed mushy broccoli, you are not alone. I'm all about making broccoli bold and bringing big spices to the party, as well as using the unique texture of its florets to create incredible taco fillings and dips. Crudité platters are banned from this book, but I will let you dunk paprika-spiced broccoli in chipotle cheese sauce! This is how I eat my broccoli and it's even better than you can imagine.

Recipe List

Buffalo Cauliflower

MAKES 4 SMALL OR 2 LARGE SERVINGS

10-in-30 | FF | 500↓

I recently lost my friend Kelly Jo to warmer weather and the countryside. Before she went off to live her dream life in the mountains, we shared one last meal. We reminisced about late nights bartending together and early breakfasts watching the sun come up. We laughed, cried, and ate Buffalo Cauliflower. There's nothing like snacking on a big plate of "wings" while talking a mile a minute and in the end feeling good about what you ate. And with a topping of blue cheese and shaved celery these guys are downright addictive. If only the "wings" and that day could last forever.

1 medium head cauliflower (about 2 pounds)

2 tablespoons olive oil

1½ teaspoons kosher salt

4 tablespoons (½ stick) unsalted butter, cut into pieces

⅓ cup Frank's RedHot Original Cayenne Pepper Sauce

1 tablespoon distilled white vinegar

¼ teaspoon Worcestershire sauce

1 cup very thinly sliced celery

½ cup crumbled blue cheese

1. Preheat the oven to 450°F.

2. Break the cauliflower into large florets and put in a large bowl. Add the oil and 1 teaspoon of the salt and toss to coat. Spread the cauliflower out evenly on a rimmed baking sheet. Bake until tender and browned, 15 to 20 minutes. Return the cauliflower to the large bowl.

3. Meanwhile, put the butter, hot sauce, vinegar, Worcestershire sauce, and the remaining ½ teaspoon salt in a small saucepan. Cook over medium heat, stirring occasionally, until the butter has melted and the Buffalo sauce has come together, 2 to 3 minutes.

4. Pour the sauce over the cauliflower and toss until well coated. Serve, dividing the celery and blue cheese equally over the portions.

FF
People, kids included, will devour anything that is smothered in Buffalo sauce and cheese. To tone down the spice for tender palates, make the sauce with ¼ cup hot sauce and ⅓ cup butter. You can also swap the blue cheese for feta, goat cheese, queso fresco, or chunks of cheddar.

IMMERSION BLENDER: A NO-MESS BEST

Let's face it, the worst part of cooking is the cleanup. And until a supersmart cleaning robot is invented to follow you around the kitchen, you are going to have to be the smart one if you are going to save yourself from the mess. Step 1 to a less messy life is to get yourself an immersion blender. A countertop blender is well and good, but an immersion blender can be a godsend. Instead of pre-cariously transferring hot liquids from your pot to your blender, spilling half on the way, blending, and then transferring everything back to the pot, you can simply put the end of the immersion blender into the pot and blend away. The cleanup? Simply rinse it off— minimal mess, and your soups and sauces are perfectly pureed.

Sandwiches,
Tacos +
The Like

Tacos

Broccoli Tacos

MAKES 4 SERVINGS

FF | 50/50

I didn't always love broccoli, I'll admit it: We had a bumpy relationship at first. But how can anyone fall in love with this green goddess when she is often treated so poorly? To make broccoli shine there are many things you can do: Roasting it, which gives it a bit of a charred, smoky flavor, is a good start. Pairing it with meaty, sweet, roasted garlic and caramelized onions for depth of flavor is also smart. And balancing all that with tart, acidic pomegranate seeds and juicy tomatoes? Well that is just plain genius! And then, why not wrap it all in a taco! Because who doesn't love tacos?! And who won't love broccoli when it's served like this?!

1 garlic bulb

3 tablespoons olive oil

Kosher salt

Ground black pepper

2 bunches broccoli

2 tablespoons unsalted butter

2 Vidalia onions, finely chopped

2 sweet or hot Italian sausages

Finely grated zest and juice of 1 lemon

½ cup grated Parmesan cheese

¼ cup sour cream

½ teaspoon smoked paprika

1 pint cherry tomatoes, halved

One 15-ounce can chickpeas, rinsed and drained

¼ cup toasted pine nuts (see Appendix, page 261)

¼ cup finely chopped scallions

¼ cup pomegranate seeds (see Appendix, page 261)

4 medium-large flour tortillas

1. Preheat the oven to 400°F.

2. Cut off the top third of the garlic bulb, exposing all the cloves on the remainder; discard the top and place the remainder, cut side up, on a square of aluminum foil. Drizzle 1 tablespoon of the oil over the

Broccoli Tacos

Green Pepper Tacos
+ Pineapple Salsa (p. 97)

Mushroom + Steak Tacos
with Corn Salsa (p. 99)

cut surface and then sprinkle salt and pepper over the top. Wrap the foil around the garlic, making sure it doesn't touch the cut surface, and seal tightly. Cut off and discard most of the main broccoli stem. Then cut the head into roughly 1-inch pieces and spread them out on a rimmed baking sheet. Drizzle with the remaining 2 tablespoons oil. Place both items in the oven; roast the broccoli until tender and charred around the edges, 30 to 40 minutes, and the garlic until golden brown and soft, 45 to 60 minutes. Transfer the broccoli to a food processor. Add the garlic, squeezing it out of its skins as you do this.

3. Meanwhile, melt the butter in a large skillet over medium-low heat. Add the onions and cook, stirring only occasionally, until lightly caramelized, about 45 minutes, or as long as it takes for your garlic to roast. Remove the skillet from the heat and set aside.

4. At the same time, heat a medium skillet over medium heat. Remove the sausages from their casing and crumble them into the heated skillet. Cook the sausage meat, breaking up with a wooden spoon, until cooked through, 3 to 5 minutes. Set aside.

5. Add the onions to the food processor with the broccoli and garlic; do not wash the skillet. Pulse the vegetables until coarsely chopped; then spoon them back into the skillet. Add the lemon zest and lemon juice to the vegetables in the skillet along with the Parmesan, sour cream, 1½ teaspoons salt, ½ teaspoon pepper, and the paprika, stirring well. Cook over low heat for 5 minutes to combine the flavors and melt the cheese. Gently stir in the tomatoes and chickpeas and cook until heated through, about 3 minutes more.

6. Meanwhile, toast the tortillas until just slightly charred by holding them with tongs over a gas burner flame or by placing them under the broiler for 15 to 30 seconds per side.

7. Spoon the filling along the middle of each tortilla, dividing it equally. Top with some of the sausage and divide the scallions, pine nuts, and pomegranate seeds equally over each serving. Fold up and eat!

Keep It Simple

- If you're in a rush, instead of caramelizing the onions, save a step by tossing peeled and quartered onions with the broccoli on the baking sheet and roasting them together in the oven.
- I like these tacos topped with scallions and pomegranate seeds for a little bite and acidity, but you may use your favorite taco toppings or no topping at all.
- You can always take the seeds out of a pomegranate yourself (see Appendix, page 261) but most grocery stores sell the seeds in small tubs in the produce section, next to the precut fruits and veggies, so take a look there for a great time-saver that saves you the mess, too.

50/50

The sausage is totally optional and acts as garnish. Simply omit it for tacos you want to be vegetarian, no need to add anything else.

FF

Think your kids are going to run from these broccoli bombs? Well try this approach: Take the filling and the sausage and make it into a quesadilla, adding a little shredded cheddar. You can make the taco version for yourself and this version for your kids and make everyone happy.

Green Pepper Tacos + Pineapple Salsa

MAKES 4 SERVINGS; ABOUT 2 CUPS SALSA

500↓ | FF | 50/50

The Pineapple Salsa adds a lightness and a freshness to the savory and smoky flavors of the meat and peppers. It provides a juiciness and acidity that is very different from the flavors in the filling yet completely complementary. So don't skip the topping! And hey, if you're strapped for time, pick up some salsa from the store and add pineapple pieces to it. There's no shame in that.

Pineapple Salsa

1 cup finely chopped fresh pineapple

½ cup finely chopped red onion

¼ cup finely chopped cored and seeded green bell pepper

½ serrano or jalapeño chile, seeds and ribs removed, finely chopped

Juice of ½ lime

¼ teaspoon kosher salt

¼ cup chopped fresh cilantro

Green Pepper Tacos

1 tablespoon olive oil, plus more if needed

1 teaspoon kosher salt

¼ teaspoon ground black pepper

2 boneless or bone-in chicken thighs (¾ pound or 1 pound), skin removed

3 large green bell peppers, cored and seeded, sliced lengthwise into ½-inch-wide strips

2 garlic cloves, minced

1 teaspoon ancho chili powder

¼ teaspoon smoked paprika

4 medium-large flour tortillas

1 cup canned black beans, rinsed and drained

½ cup crumbled feta cheese (large pieces, about 2 ounces)

Pineapple Salsa

Put the pineapple, onion, bell pepper, serrano, lime juice, and salt in a medium bowl and stir until combined. Stir in the cilantro. Let the salsa sit at room temperature while you make the taco filling.

Green Pepper Tacos

1. Preheat the oven to 450°F. Heat the oil in a large, oven-safe skillet over medium-high heat. While it is heating, sprinkle ½ teaspoon of the salt and the black pepper over the chicken thighs. When the oil is shimmering, add the chicken to the skillet and cook, undisturbed, until golden brown on the bottom, 3 to 5 minutes. Flip the chicken thighs over and cook the opposite side until golden brown, 3 to 5 minutes more. Transfer the skillet to the oven and bake the chicken until it is cooked through, 10 to 15 minutes.

2. Remove the skillet from the oven and transfer the chicken to a plate. Place the skillet back on the burner, this time over medium heat, adding more oil if needed for sautéing the bell peppers. Add the bell peppers, stir in the remaining ½ teaspoon salt, and cook until slightly tender, about 5 minutes. Stir in the garlic, chili powder, and paprika and cook until the bell peppers are tender, 3 to 5 minutes more.

3. Meanwhile, shred the chicken. Toast the tortillas until just slightly charred by holding them with tongs over a gas burner flame or by placing them under the broiler for 15 to 30 seconds per side.

4. When the peppers are cooked, add the chicken and beans to the skillet and stir to combine. Cook until the beans are warmed through, 1 to 2 minutes.

5. Spoon the bell pepper mixture onto the tortillas, dividing it equally. Add a spoonful of the salsa to each taco, and scatter some feta over the top. Fold up and enjoy!

Keep It Simple

• You can make the Pineapple Salsa ahead of time as the longer it sits the better it gets.
• Swap the chili powder and paprika for a packet of taco seasoning mixed with a splash of water.
• You can also use white meat chicken or even pork or steak if you prefer.

FF

If your kids like tacos, they will love these. If you want them to focus more on the chicken than the peppers, chop the peppers into a small dice instead of the long strips, and use whatever toppings they prefer.

50/50

Add another pepper and cup of beans, but use only 1 chicken thigh and cook it separately. Then when you assemble the tacos, add the chicken to only two.

Mushroom + Steak Tacos with Corn Salsa

MAKES 4 ENTRÉE-SIZE TACOS; ABOUT 2 CUPS SALSA

500↓ | 50/50

Even before my food revolution, I enjoyed countless tacos. Although my diet contained no vegetables, meat, or beans, I could enjoy tacos by ordering like this: one taco, no beans, no veggies, no meat, extra cheese. After a quizzical look from the server, I'd be handed a tortilla packed with cheese and sometimes a little iceberg lettuce—yep, lettuce! I was really living on the edge. Luckily, my vision of what makes a good taco has changed a bit since then. Now tacos to me are just plain fun, like these Mushroom + Steak Tacos, where tasty veggies add layers of flavors and a little meat goes a long way.

Corn Salsa

2 ears corn

1 large tomato, finely chopped

½ cup finely chopped scallions

¼ cup coarsely chopped fresh cilantro, plus a few whole leaves for garnish

Juice of 2 limes

2 teaspoons kosher salt

Mushroom + Steak Tacos

2 poblano chiles

½ teaspoon chipotle chili powder

½ teaspoon ancho chili powder

½ teaspoon garlic powder

½ teaspoon smoked paprika

1 teaspoon kosher salt

One 8-ounce flank steak

2 tablespoons olive oil, plus more as needed

3 portobello mushroom caps, cut into ¼-inch-thick slices

4 medium-large flour tortillas

1 cup crumbled queso fresco (4 ounces)

Corn Salsa

1. Preheat a gas or charcoal grill (or preheat a grill pan over medium-high heat). Husk the corn. When the grill is hot, place the corn ears on the rack and cook until slightly charred on all sides, about 5 minutes, turning as needed. Let the ears cool; then slice off the kernels and put them in a small bowl.

2. Add the tomato, scallions, cilantro, lime juice, and salt to the bowl with the corn and stir to mix well. Let the salsa sit at room temperature while you make the taco filling; it will taste best if it sits for at least 30 minutes.

Mushroom + Steak Tacos

1. Use the grill, a broiler, or the gas burner on the stovetop to char the poblanos: Simply place them over the burner or under the broiler heat source (use tongs if you're working on the stovetop) and cook until they are mostly black on all sides, 5 to 8 minutes, turning as needed. Put the poblanos in a plastic food storage bag and seal the bag. When the poblanos are cool enough to handle, rub off the skins with a paper towel. Cut the poblanos open lengthwise, remove the stem and seeds, and cut the poblanos into long strips.

2. To make a spice rub, whisk together the chipotle and ancho chili powders, garlic powder, paprika, and salt in a small bowl. Rub half this mixture over all sides of the steak.

3. Heat the oil in a large skillet over high heat. Add the steak and cook until medium rare, 3 to 5 minutes per side. Transfer the steak to a cutting board. Reduce the heat to medium; if the skillet is too dry for sautéing, add a bit more oil. Stir in the mushrooms and the remaining half of the spice rub and cook until the mushrooms are brown and tender, about 5 minutes.

4. Meanwhile, toast the tortillas until just slightly charred by holding them with tongs over a burner with a gas flame or by placing them under the broiler for 15 to 30 seconds per side. When the mushrooms are cooked, add the poblanos to the skillet, stir, and cook to heat through, 1 to 2 minutes more.

5. Cut the steak into ¼-inch-thick slices. Spoon the mushroom mixture onto the tortillas, dividing it equally. Add one-quarter of the steak and a scoop of the Corn Salsa to each. Scatter some queso fresco and a few cilantro leaves or parsley over the top. Fold up and serve immediately.

Keep It Simple

- If you can't find the poblano chiles, replace them with Anaheim chiles or even regular bell peppers.
- To save some time, you can sauté the chiles in the pan with the mushrooms instead of roasting them.
- Use cheddar, Monterey Jack, feta, or even fresh mozzarella instead.
- Use less expensive mushrooms—common white button mushrooms work almost as well as portobellos.
- It's fine to replace the ancho and chipotle chili powders with regular chili powder or a package of taco seasoning.
- Grilling fresh ears of corn gives a slight charred flavor to the dish, but to save time use frozen, thawed corn kernels.

50/50

- To make half the servings (2 tacos) vegetarian, use just 4 ounces of steak and a total of 4 portobello caps. Divide the spice rub accordingly and cook the steak in a separate skillet!
- To make a totally meatless version, skip the steak and use 5 portobello caps. Also add some sliced avocado to the taco when assembling if you like.

Baby Spinach, Orange + Salmon Pitas
with Tzatziki

MAKES 4 SANDWICHES; ABOUT 2 CUPS SAUCE

As adults many of us lunch on whatever is available in our office cafeteria or a nearby deli, leaving the idea of homemade far behind. But remember when you used to take a lunch to school? Well, you still can! When I first made this sandwich for my friend Liz, she remarked that she would eat it every day for lunch if she could. She was onto something! The salmon is great warm, at room temperature, or cold, the tzatziki provides a luscious satisfying creaminess, and the oranges bring in a fruity, vitamin C–rich twist. All this, wrapped in a pita, and you've got an easy-to-pack, one-handed super lunch. I see you smiling. This is what it feels like to love lunch again.

Tzatziki Sauce

1 cup Greek yogurt

Juice of 1 lemon

¾ cup finely chopped, seeded cucumber

1 small garlic clove, grated

2 teaspoons finely chopped fresh dill

2 teaspoons finely chopped fresh mint

½ teaspoon kosher salt

¼ teaspoon ground black pepper

Spinach, Orange + Salmon Pitas

3 oranges

1 pound salmon fillet (wild-caught is best)

½ teaspoon kosher salt

¼ teaspoon ground black pepper

1 tablespoon olive oil

4 pita breads

4 cups packed fresh spinach

1 cup canned white beans, rinsed and drained

Tzatziki Sauce

Whisk together the yogurt and lemon juice in a small bowl. Stir in the cucumber, garlic, dill, mint, salt, and pepper until combined. Cover and refrigerate while you bake the salmon.

Spinach, Orange + Salmon Pitas

1. Preheat the oven to 375°F.

2. Cut 1 orange into ¼-inch-thick rounds. Peel the 2 remaining oranges and separate them into segments.

3. Lay a large piece of aluminum foil on a baking sheet. Arrange half the orange slices in the center and lay the salmon on top of them. Sprinkle the salmon with the salt and pepper and drizzle with the oil. Arrange the remaining orange slices over the salmon. Make the foil into a sealed package by folding up and crimping together the long edges and then folding each end up and over on itself, enclosing the salmon.

4. Bake the salmon in the preheated oven until it is just cooked through and flakes with a fork, 15 to 30 minutes depending on its thickness. Meanwhile, cut each of the pitas in half, forming 2 equal pockets.

5. When the salmon is done, spread a healthy smear of the Tzatziki Sauce inside each pita pocket. Flake the salmon into small pieces and divide them equally among the pockets, along with the orange segments, spinach, and beans. Serve right away; two pita halves per diner.

Keep It Simple

- Make the tzatziki several hours ahead or even the night before if possible. The flavors will marry and intensify as it sits.
- Why not make enough for a whole week of lunches? Just keep the sauce on the side and wrap all the pitas individually in foil.
- You could also serve this in a wrap or tortilla instead of a pita.
- The mint ramps up the flavor of the tzatziki but you can use just dill for a more traditional take on the sauce.

Red Cabbage + Raspberry Grilled Cheese

MAKES 2 SANDWICHES

10-in-20 | FF

My husband likes to tell stories of his best friend Max's late night cooking extravaganzas when they were younger. Max was a great, but messy cook. If only they had known how simple it was to make a sophisticated grilled cheese with virtually no mess. This grilled cheese has it all—gooey melted cheese, hot crunchy buttered bread, and a sweet and tart filling that breaks up the rich layers of fontina. The sautéed cabbage with raspberry jam provides a little extra crunch along with sweetness and color that makes people stop and take notice. So blast the *Top Gun* anthem, open a cold beer, and dive right in!

2 tablespoons olive oil

6 cups lightly packed shredded purple cabbage (12 ounces)

1 teaspoon kosher salt

¼ cup raspberry jam

¼ cup champagne vinegar

8 ounces fontina cheese, sliced

4 slices sourdough bread

2 tablespoons unsalted butter, at room temperature

1. Heat the oil in a large skillet over medium heat. Stir in the cabbage and salt and cook until tender but not mushy, 3 to 4 minutes. Stir in the jam and vinegar and cook until most of the liquid has evaporated and the cabbage is completely tender, 2 to 3 minutes more. Remove the skillet from the heat.

2. Heat a second large skillet over medium-low heat. Butter 1 side of each slice of bread. Place 2 pieces of bread, butter side down, on a plate. Top each with 3 alternating layers: first of cheese, then cabbage, and then the rest of the cheese, dividing them equally, then finish off with another slice of bread, butter side up. Place the sandwiches in the skillet and cook them until browned on the bottom, 3 to 5 minutes. Flip them over and cook until the other side has browned and the cheese has melted, 3 to 5 minutes more, gently pressing the sandwiches as they cook. Cut in half and serve.

Portobello "Cheesesteaks"
with Provolone Cheese Sauce

MAKES 4 SANDWICHES; ABOUT 2 CUPS SAUCE

Make It Meaty

A cheesesteak is not exactly something that you can simply revamp by upping the amount of veggies and toning down the meat. There aren't really any veggies in it to begin with. It is, after all, just a whole lot of meat topped with cheese, and that's about it. Now the classic can be quite tasty, but as I may have mentioned, I prefer my meat . . . on the side. So, true to form, I took the cheesesteak and turned it on its head, with mushrooms and caramelized onions, and without sacrificing the cheese. It may not replace the original, but this little guy deserves to be the signature dish of some city. Submit your applications now.

Provolone Cheese Sauce

1 tablespoon unsalted butter

1 tablespoon all-purpose flour

1 cup whole milk

¾ cup shredded provolone cheese (3 ounces)

½ cup grated Parmesan cheese (2 ounces)

¼ teaspoon ground black pepper

Kosher salt, if needed

Portobello Cheesesteak Sandwiches

4 tablespoons (½ stick) unsalted butter

2 large Vidalia onions, thinly sliced

3 teaspoons kosher salt

6 garlic cloves, minced

3 teaspoons minced fresh rosemary leaves

2 bay leaves

8 large portobello mushroom caps (about 1½ pounds), cut into ¼-inch-thick slices

2 tablespoons red wine vinegar

2 tablespoons Worcestershire sauce

Four 6-inch baguettes or sandwich rolls

¼ cup finely chopped red onion

Provolone Cheese Sauce

Melt the butter in a small saucepan over medium heat. Whisk in the flour and cook for 1 minute. Whisk in the milk, and continue to whisk until there are no lumps. Cook, whisking occasionally, until the mixture has bubbled and thickened, 3 to 5 minutes. Add the provolone, and whisk until it has melted and incorporated. Add the Parmesan and continue to whisk until it has melted and combined. Whisk in the pepper; taste the sauce and add a pinch of salt if you like. Keep the sauce warm over low heat while you make the sandwiches.

Portobello Cheesesteak Sandwiches

1. Melt 3 tablespoons of the butter in a large skillet over medium heat. Add the Vidalia onions and 1 teaspoon of the salt and cook for 10 minutes, stirring frequently. Reduce the heat to medium-low, stir in the garlic, rosemary, and bay leaves, and cook until the onions are golden brown and caramelized, stirring only occasionally, 35 to 40 minutes more.

2. Transfer the onion mixture to a small bowl and remove and discard the bay leaves. Add the remaining 1 tablespoon butter to the skillet and let it melt. Add the mushrooms, increase the heat to medium-high, and cook until the mushrooms are golden brown and tender but not mushy, about 5 minutes. Return the onion mixture to the skillet and stir in the vinegar, Worcestershire sauce, and the remaining 2 teaspoons salt; cook for 3 minutes more.

3. Meanwhile, slice the baguettes so they lie open like a book. To assemble the sandwiches, divide the mushroom mixture equally, placing it over the baguettes. Top with the Provolone Cheese Sauce and the chopped red onion. Serve hot and gooey!

Keep It Simple

• The caramelized onions add a depth of flavor and meatiness to this dish, but they do take a while to cook. To make this dish super speedy, simply sauté the onions just until they are tender, 7 to 10 minutes, and then add an extra teaspoon of Worcestershire sauce in step 2.
• You can use provolone cheese slices instead of the shredded, just use about 3 oz.

Make It Meaty

Replace half the mushrooms with 6 ounces of steak for a meatier "cheesesteak" that is still well balanced.

Burned Carrot Sandwich
with Cannellini Bean Spread

MAKES 2 SANDWICHES; 1½ CUPS SPREAD (ENOUGH SPREAD FOR 6 SANDWICHES)

500↓ | FF | Make It Meaty

I'm not a huge fan of carrots; I still cringe a little when I see people snacking on raw carrots. But there are always tricks to get a new vegetable into your routine: Today that trick is to burn them! Carrots have more sugar than the average vegetable, so when you roast them until they are burnt a bit, all shriveled and mostly black, all these sugars caramelize to completely change the texture and taste. For me this turns the carrot from inedible to totally crave worthy. So this is how I eat my carrots and, mixed on a sandwich with this creamy cannellini and goat cheese spread, it may be the only way you'll ever want to eat carrots again.

Burned Carrot Sandwich

1 small cucumber

1½ pounds baby carrots

1½ tablespoons olive oil

¾ teaspoon kosher salt

1 teaspoon smoked paprika

Two 6-inch baguettes, sliced in half lengthwise, or
    6- to 8-inch sandwich rolls

½ cup alfalfa sprouts

Cannellini Bean Spread

One 15-ounce can cannellini beans, rinsed and
    drained

4 ounces soft goat cheese

¼ cup lightly packed fresh flat-leaf parsley leaves

Juice of ½ lemon

1 garlic clove

1 teaspoon kosher salt

1 teaspoon minced fresh rosemary leaves

2 tablespoons extra-virgin olive oil

Burned Carrot Sandwich

1. Preheat the oven to 425°F.

2. Cut the cucumber into twenty-four ⅛-inch-thick rounds and set aside. If the carrots are wet, pat them dry. Toss the carrots with the oil, salt, and smoked paprika in a medium bowl; then spread them out on a

Burned Carrot Sandwich

Celeriac + Lobster Rolls (p. 111)

rimmed baking sheet. Bake in the preheated oven until very charred and slightly shriveled, about 60 minutes, stirring occasionally. While the carrots are baking, make the Cannellini Bean Spread (below).

3. Assemble the sandwiches: Spread 2 tablespoons of the Cannellini Bean Spread over the cut surface of each baguette half. Top each bottom half with a layer of cucumber, then a layer of carrots, and finally the sprouts, dividing everything equally. Put the top baguette half on each sandwich, and enjoy!

Cannellini Bean Spread

Put the beans, cheese, parsley, lemon juice, garlic, salt, and rosemary in a food processor and process until smooth. Then, with the machine running, stream in the oil and process until combined.

Serving Suggestions!

I'm always glad that this recipe makes more bean spread than is needed for the two sandwiches. Just store it in the fridge and use it on your go-to, cold-cuts sandwich or toss it with cooked veggies. It's also great served as a dip. Too much is NOT too much.

Keep It Simple

- You can use any green or sprout you like on this sandwich. I like alfalfa sprouts because of their unique texture and crunch, but baby arugula, baby spinach, or watercress would all work.
- Replace the smoked paprika with regular paprika or chili powder if you like.

FF

If you want to hide the carrots in the sandwich from your kids, puree them up with the Cannellini Bean Spread. Adding some meat from the "Make It Meaty" tip can help this version feel more complete, with a bit more texture.

Make It Meaty

Try some Breaded Chicken (see page 154) or grilled chicken on this sandwich. Tiny Chicken Meatballs (page 223) also add a nice richness with a bit more flavor. Or go in a different direction and try canned tuna for a tuna salad–inspired version.

Celeriac + Lobster Rolls
Topped with Fennel + Apple Slaw

MAKES 4 SANDWICHES

My good friend Kelly came over and watered my 60 plus plants recently while I was in Germany. A big thank-you was in order so I decided to make a decadent, fresh, and totally unique lunch on my terrace. A hot lobster roll popped into my head. As good as that is, I knew I wanted to do more with it. In many lobster salads you find celery, so it made sense to me to include celeriac, the knobby root of a particular variety of celery. When caramelized it adds a meaty, smoky depth of flavor that makes this a lobster roll that really satisfies. Add some fresh apples and fennel to break it all up and give it a refreshing bite, and THAT is how I say "Thank you."

Fennel + Apple Slaw

1 small fennel bulb, very thinly sliced (about 1½ cups)

1 Red Delicious apple, cut into long, thin strips

1 jalapeño chile or Fresno chile, seeds and ribs removed, minced

Juice of 1 lemon

Juice of ½ orange

½ teaspoon kosher salt

Basil + Lemon Aioli

1 large egg yolk

1 teaspoon Dijon mustard

1 small garlic clove

1 tablespoon white wine vinegar

1 teaspoon kosher salt

Finely grated zest of ½ lemon

Juice of 1 lemon

½ cup vegetable oil

¼ cup finely chopped fresh basil leaves

Celeriac + Lobster Rolls

1 tablespoon olive oil

1 celeriac (1½ to 2 pounds), peeled and cut into ¼-inch cubes

1 teaspoon kosher salt

2 tablespoons unsalted butter

4 split-top hot dog rolls

9 ounces fresh cooked lobster meat (equivalent to one 3-pound lobster), coarsely chopped

Fennel + Apple Slaw

Mix the fennel, apples, jalapeño, lemon juice, orange juice, and salt in a large bowl, stirring until well combined. Set aside on the countertop to let the fennel and apples soften while you prepare the rest of the sandwich.

Aioli

Add the egg yolk, vinegar, lemon zest, lemon juice, mustard, garlic, and salt to a blender and blend on high for 10 seconds. Leave the blender on and *very* slowly drizzle in the oil, starting with a couple drops and adding more as you go until the aioli is thick. Scrape the thickened aioli into a small bowl and stir in the basil. Set aside.

Celeriac + Lobster Rolls

1. Heat the oil in a large skillet over medium-high heat. Stir in the celeriac, sprinkle with the salt, and stir again. Cook until the celeriac is tender and browned on all sides, 10 to 12 minutes.

2. Meanwhile, melt the butter in a second large skillet or a griddle over medium heat. Add the rolls and cook until browned on the sides, 2 to 4 minutes.

3. As soon as the celeriac is cooked, reduce the heat to low and stir the lobster into the skillet. Cook until warmed through, 2 to 3 minutes. Remove the skillet from the heat. Add the aioli and stir until well combined.

4. Spoon the lobster mixture into the rolls, dividing it equally. Top each roll with one-quarter of the slaw.

Keep It Simple

- If you're not in the mood to make your own aioli, skip it and use ¾ cup mayonnaise instead, adding the basil, a squeeze of lemon juice, and a little grated garlic.
- Fennel has a nice licorice flavor, but can be replaced with a small red onion or cabbage in a pinch. If you have some tarragon on hand add it when using these substitutes.
- Go ahead, make the slaw in advance. You'll get a jump on the prep and the longer it sits, the better it gets.
- For simpler slaw use, ¼ teaspoon crushed red pepper flakes instead of the hot pepper, and just lemon juice instead of both juices.
- Make this meal a bit more accessible by substituting shrimp for the lobster. Or for a different take on things, chopped chicken breast makes for one heck of a tasty sandwich, too!

Roasted Broccoli, Corn + Green Chile–Stuffed Naan

MAKES 2 SERVINGS; DOUBLE THE RECIPE AS YOU WISH

10-in-20 | FF | Make It Meaty

Naan bread is tasty . . . OK, I assume you're looking for me to describe it as more than "tasty." Naan is an Indian bread that, like a pita, has a large hollow center, created by the moisture in its dough turning to steam and forming an air pocket when it bakes. But unlike pita, naan is chewy and delicate in flavor and texture and, once again, very tasty! Besides stuffing it like I do here, you can use naan as the base for a flatbread or pizza, or cut it up for dipping in my Beet Hummus (page 37) or Broccoli + Feta Dip (page 39). However you prepare it, it's sure to be (you guessed it) TASTY!

1½ cups broccoli florets

¾ teaspoon kosher salt

1 teaspoon plus 2 tablespoons olive oil

⅓ cup corn kernels

1½ cups shredded Pepper Jack cheese

Half a 4-ounce can chopped green chiles

1 naan

½ teaspoon ground turmeric

1. Turn on the broiler to high, if you have that option. Place broccoli, salt, and oil in a food processor, pulse until finely chopped and then spread on a baking sheet and place under the broiler until charred and tender, 3 to 5 minutes.

2. Return the broccoli to the medium bowl. Add the corn to the broccoli, along with the cheese, the remaining ¼ teaspoon salt, and the chiles and stir to combine.

3. Very gently open the naan by running a knife along one edge between the layers, creating a pocket. Naan usually has one layer that is thicker than the other, so try not to rip the thin layer. If some tearing occurs, that's OK—the filling should stay in and the cheese will act as a glue, sealing up the bread as it cooks.

4. Gently spoon the broccoli mixture into the naan. You want to push it to the edges, but if you are having trouble getting the filling into a particular spot, don't worry, it will melt into those areas—it doesn't need to be perfect.

5. Briefly heat the remaining 2 tablespoons oil in a large skillet over medium heat. Stir in the turmeric, making sure it spreads evenly through the oil. Lay the naan in the skillet and cook until crisp and golden brown on the bottom, about 3 minutes. Gently turn it over and cook the opposite side until it is golden brown and the cheese inside has melted, about 3 minutes more. Cut the naan into sixths or quarters and serve immediately.

Keep It Simple

- Though most stores are carrying naan bread these days, there are lots of substitutes that you can use for this recipe if it's hard to find: Pita works very nicely, you can use two tortillas and make it like a quesadilla, or use the filling in between two slices of regular loaf bread, creating an outrageous grilled cheese.
- Turmeric has a warm, peppery flavor and adds a great bright yellow color to the dish, but it can successfully be replaced with paprika or garlic powder or simply omitted.
- Green chiles come in a small can and can usually be found next to the refried beans, taco sauce, and tortillas in your grocery store.
- Instead of buying frozen corn kernels or corn in a can, use the kernels from one ear of fresh corn. Simply put the husked ear in boiling water for 5 minutes or better yet, put it on your grill until slightly charred. Use a sharp knife to cut down the side of the ear to remove the kernels.

FF

Nothing like hiding broccoli in cheese and between some bread to get your kids to gobble it up. But if the spice from the Pepper Jack cheese is too much for them, replace it with mozzarella or cheddar.

Make It Meaty

Add 2 ounces of very finely chopped cooked chicken to the filling mixture. Or, to add an extra protein kick without the meat, add ¼ cup very finely chopped edamame.

Pumpkin Quesadilla

MAKES ONE 8-INCH QUESADILLA; 2 SERVINGS

FF | 50/50

My niece Lucy LOVES quesadillas almost as much as she loves chocolate. But her idea of a delicious quesadilla is made up of two things and two things only, a tortilla and cheese (sounds like a girl named "Picky Nikki" I used to know ;)). Tortillas and cheese are a good foundation, but when you ramp up the flavor with a creamy and spicy pumpkin-and-green-chile filling and top everything with extra cheese, crunchy pumpkin seeds, and a simple salad, well now we are really talking about a great night. Plus, you can get all of this to the table in under 20 minutes. It looks like your Tuesday night just got a lot more interesting.

Salad Topping

1 cup sliced romaine lettuce strips (¼-inch-wide)

¼ cup quartered cherry tomatoes

Juice of ½ lime

1 teaspoon olive oil

Pinch of kosher salt

Pumpkin Quesadilla

One 4½-ounce can chopped green chiles

½ cup 100 percent pure pumpkin puree

2 tablespoons finely chopped fresh cilantro

1 teaspoon sriracha sauce

½ teaspoon kosher salt

2 medium flour tortillas (8 inches)

1 cup shredded sharp cheddar cheese (4 ounces)

⅓ cup finely chopped cooked chicken (2 ounces)

2 tablespoons olive oil

½ cup shredded mozzarella cheese

2 tablespoons shelled, unsalted, raw pumpkin seeds

Salad Topping

Toss the lettuce, tomatoes, lime juice, oil, and salt in a small bowl. Set aside while you make the quesadilla.

Pumpkin Quesadilla

1. Preheat the oven to 400°F.

2. Put the chiles in a small bowl. Pat them gently with a paper towel to absorb some of the liquid. Add the pumpkin, cilantro, sriracha, and salt to the bowl and stir until combined.

3. Lay one tortilla on a plate. Scatter half the cheddar over it, and spoon the pumpkin mixture evenly over the cheese. Scatter the chicken and then the remaining cheddar over the pumpkin mixture. Lay the second tortilla on top.

4. Heat the oil in a large oven-safe skillet. Transfer the quesadilla to the skillet and cook until the bottom tortilla has browned on the underside and crisp, about 3 minutes. Flip the quesadilla over and cook the opposite side the same way, about 3 minutes more.

5. Remove the skillet from the heat. Spread the mozzarella evenly over the quesadilla and sprinkle the pumpkin seeds on top. Place the skillet in the oven and cook until the mozzarella has melted and the seeds are lightly toasted, about 5 minutes. Top with the salad, cut into wedges, and serve hot!

Keep It Simple

- I always have lots of cheese in my fridge, like LOTS, and for this recipe two types of cheese seemed nice, and I liked the color difference. But you can easily use all cheddar instead of a mix.
- The seeds on top give such a great texture to the quesadilla, it's my favorite part, and since you can almost always find pumpkin seeds, AKA *pepitas*, in the bulk section of your grocery store, you can get just the amount you need.
- Sriracha is a great hot sauce, but whatever variety is your favorite is perfect for this.
- I love having cooked chicken in the freezer, that way I always have 2 ounces worth ready to go for this quesadilla.
- Strictly speaking this doesn't qualify as a 10-in-20 recipe—a few too many ingredients! But it comes together really quickly, making it the perfect lunch or easy dinner.

FF

With the pumpkin being the same color as the cheese, this kind of just looks like a big cheese quesadilla that everyone is bound to love. You can also use a little extra cheese and a little less pumpkin. And though I love the seeds on top, they can always be left off.

50/50

Sometimes I use just 1 ounce of cooked chicken for my husband's side of the quesadilla and leave my side chicken-free for a great 50/50 meal.

Mushroom + Beef Sloppy Joes

MAKES 4 SANDWICHES

500↓ | FF | 50/50

My father in-law, Bob, is a fantastic cook and the epitome of a "meat eater"—he's never seen a piece of beef or pork that didn't have his name on it. As you may imagine he can be weary of my *Meat on the Side* meals, especially ones that put cabbage on nachos or make cauliflower into a "wing." So when serving him these sloppy Joes I "neglected" to mention that half of the filling was mushrooms. With the thick and tangy sauce you would never know, and guess what, he didn't. I got the "very good, Nikki," his highest compliment, and I immediately knew that this recipe was "book worthy." After all it's Bob approved, and that is no small feat.

1 tablespoon olive oil, plus more if needed

8 ounces ground sirloin

1 pound portobello mushrooms, stems discarded, caps finely chopped

1 small green bell pepper, cored, seeded, and finely chopped

1 small yellow onion, finely chopped

1½ teaspoons kosher salt

¼ teaspoon ground black pepper

One 8-ounce can tomato sauce

3 tablespoons Worcestershire sauce

2 tablespoons molasses

2 tablespoons white wine vinegar

1 tablespoon sriracha or other hot sauce

3 tablespoons tomato paste

1 teaspoon minced fresh thyme leaves

4 hamburger buns

Finely chopped dill pickles, for serving

Sliced pickled banana peppers, for serving

1. Heat the oil in a large deep skillet over medium-high heat. Add the sirloin, breaking up with a spoon or spatula, and cook until it has browned, about 5 minutes. Then, if the skillet is too dry for sautéing the mushrooms, add a bit more oil. Stir in the mushrooms and cook until they are brown and tender, about 5 minutes.

2. Reduce the heat to medium. Add the bell peppers, onion, ½ teaspoon of the salt, and the black pepper to the skillet and stir to combine. Cook until all the veggies are tender, 5 to 7 minutes. Meanwhile, whisk together the tomato sauce, Worcestershire sauce, molasses, vinegar, sriracha, and the remaining 1 teaspoon salt in a small bowl.

3. Add the tomato paste and thyme to the mixture in the skillet and stir to combine. Cook for 2 minutes. Then stir in the tomato sauce mixture and cook until the sauce thickens and coats the veggies and meat and all the flavors come together, 5 to 7 minutes more.

4. To serve, spoon the Sloppy Joe mixture onto the bottom half of each hamburger bun, dividing it equally, and dot with some pickles and banana peppers before adding the bun tops.

Keep It Simple

- Along with the heat it provides, sriracha has a great flavor, but any hot sauce will work. Other favorites of mine are Cholula Hot Sauce and Frank's RedHot Sauce.
- Though I like the deep, musty flavor of portobellos, any variety of mushroom can be used for this recipe—even everyday white button mushrooms will taste great.
- Haven't seen molasses in your kitchen since the last time you made gingerbread? No problem, use 3 tablespoons of brown sugar instead.

FF

This is bound to be a staple in your house and makes for great leftovers. Skip the pickles and banana peppers for those who prefer a milder flavor, and add less hot sauce for younger eaters.

50/50

- To make some servings vegetarian and some *Meat on the Side,* use about 2 ounces sirloin for each meat serving and an extra 2 to 3 ounces mushrooms for each vegetarian serving. Cook up the sirloin separately from the veggies. Add the sauce to the veggie mixture until it is well coated and serve the vegetarian portions; then add the meat and remaining sauce to the remaining veggies, stir to combine, and serve the *Meat on the Side* portions.
- To make this dish completely vegetarian, omit the ground sirloin and add an extra ½ pound of mushrooms.

Pizzas
+ Flatbreads

Brussels Sprouts + Tomatillos Skillet Pizza

MAKES ONE 12-INCH PIZZA

10-in-30 | 500↓ | Make It Meaty

I like my food to be amazing, and there are a couple of amazing things happening in this recipe. First, we are making pizza in a skillet, which is a foolproof way to create a crisp crust with a chewy and moist inside. Second, we are taking Brussels sprouts to a whole new level, separating the leaves and allowing them to get the perfect amount of "charredness" (totally a word). And last we are adding tomatillos—after peeling away their papery outer skin, we are left with what looks like green tomatoes but tastes like "apple-ish, grape-ish amazingness" (yes, totally words). I'm introducing Italy to Mexico and creating a tart, refreshing finish on an amazing pie.

¾ pound Brussels sprouts

2 teaspoons olive oil

¾ teaspoon kosher salt

1 pound pizza dough, at room temperature

1½ cups shredded Gruyère cheese (6 ounces)

2 garlic cloves, minced

2 medium-large tomatillos

2 tablespoons chopped fresh cilantro leaves

½ lime

1. Cut off the bottom stem of each Brussels sprout and then gently tear or cut the leaves away from the core; discard the very center. Put the leaves in a medium bowl; you should have about 3 cups loosely packed leaves. Stir in 1 teaspoon of the oil and ½ teaspoon of the salt.

2. Preheat the oven to 500°F.

3. Brush a 12-inch cast-iron skillet with the remaining 1 teaspoon oil. Place the dough on a lightly floured work surface and stretch or roll it to a 10-inch-diameter round. Fit the dough into the skillet, pushing it out to the edges. Scatter the cheese evenly over the dough and then sprinkle with the garlic. Scatter the Brussels sprouts leaves over the top.

4. Place the skillet over medium-high heat and cook until the underside of the dough is very lightly golden brown, about 5 minutes. Transfer the skillet to the oven and cook until the leaves are charred and the dough is cooked through, 10 to 12 minutes more.

5. Meanwhile, remove and discard the husks from the tomatillos. Wash and dry the fruit and then coarsely chop it. Put the chopped tomatillos in a small bowl and add the cilantro. Juice the lime into the bowl, add the remaining ¼ teaspoon salt, and toss to combine. Scatter the mixture over the hot pizza and serve.

Keep It Simple

- I never quite mastered making my own pizza dough, so I prefer to leave it to the professionals. Just pop into your favorite pizzeria (or supermarket) and ask them if you can buy some dough: They are happy to sell it to you and you are happy to have fantastic dough you didn't have to make.
- To make this pizza you can use 12 ounces of dough, or 15 ounces; whatever you can get your hands on, just don't use more than 1 pound as the pie will be too thick.
- Though I'm a big fan of tomatillos, they are not always easy to find, so to replace them try diced pears, apples, or red or green tomatoes.
- Gruyère can be replaced with a combination of mozzarella and Parmesan, or just mozzarella.

Make It Meaty

Crisp and chopped bacon or pancetta are great toppings that can be sprinkled on with the tomatillos. Or for something a little more substantial, 4 to 6 ounces of cooked, chopped chicken is a great addition.

Bruschetta Pizza

MAKES ONE 15-INCH PIZZA

FF

A pizza sauce is well and good, but I started thinking about a pizza where you take the tomatoes out of the sauce and put them center stage. Using them fresh and undisturbed makes a pizza that truly celebrates the tomato and is big on veggies and big on flavor. This pizza keeps things simple while at the same time ramping up the flavor with the perfect combination of ingredients. Things like tangy goat cheese and sweet yet assertive balsamic vinegar perfectly complement the ripe and juicy tomatoes, making them the best they can be. It's summer on a pizza, any time of the year.

Parmesan Sauce

2 tablespoons unsalted butter

2 tablespoons all-purpose flour

1 cup 2 percent milk

1 cup grated Parmesan cheese (4 ounces)

½ teaspoon kosher salt

⅛ teaspoon ground nutmeg

Crust + Topping

3 medium tomatoes

¼ cup balsamic vinegar

2 tablespoons chopped fresh basil leaves

1 teaspoon minced fresh thyme leaves

1 tablespoon extra-virgin olive oil

½ teaspoon kosher salt

1 pound pizza dough, at room temperature

2 tablespoons cornmeal, plus more if needed

2 ounces soft goat cheese, crumbled

Parmesan Sauce

Melt the butter in a small saucepan over medium-low heat. Whisk in the flour until well combined and cook for 2 minutes. Gradually add the milk, and continue to whisk until there are no lumps. Cook, whisking occasionally, until the mixture has bubbled and thickened, 3 to 5 minutes. Whisk in the Parmesan, salt, and nutmeg, cover the sauce, and set aside.

Crust + Topping

1. Preheat the oven to 500°F. Place a pizza stone or baking sheet in the oven to preheat.

2. While the oven is heating, chop the tomatoes. Heat the vinegar in a small saucepan over medium-low heat and cook until the vinegar is syrupy and has reduced by half, 5 to 7 minutes. While the vinegar is reducing, mix the tomatoes, basil, thyme, oil, and salt in a medium bowl and stir until well combined.

3. Roll out the dough on a lightly floured surface into a 15-inch-diameter round about ¼ inch thick. Sprinkle the cornmeal on a pizza peel or rimless baking sheet and place the dough round on it. Shake the peel or baking sheet to check that the dough will easily slide off it; if not, add more cornmeal. Spread the Parmesan sauce over the dough.

4. Open the oven, and pull out the rack, then slide the pizza onto the hot stone or sheet. Push in the rack and bake the crust until crisp and slightly brown, about 10 minutes if using the stone, or 15 minutes if using the sheet. Keep an eye on the crust as it bakes and pop any air bubbles that form with a fork.

5. Remove the pizza from the oven, transfer to a cutting board, and spread the tomato mixture over the top. Drizzle the reduced vinegar over the tomatoes, and scatter the goat cheese on top. Cut the pizza into wedges and serve immediately.

Keep It Simple

- You can buy balsamic reduction instead of reducing it yourself, or you can just use a splash of vinegar right out of the bottle. It will be more acidic than if you had reduced it, but still very tasty.
- I've used 1 percent, 2 percent, and whole milk for this recipe, and they all worked fine, so use whatever you have on hand.
- Substitute shredded or cubed mozzarella for the goat cheese if desired. If you want it melted, add it on top of the Parmesan Sauce before baking. Or for an extra layer of flavor, try Gorgonzola cheese.

FF

- For pickier eaters, try this variation: Top the pizza with the Parmesan sauce and tomato mixture, add some mozzarella cheese, and bake and serve, omitting the vinegar and goat cheese. You'll have a more classic-looking and classic-tasting pie while still getting plenty of tomato goodness.

- Sneak some extra veggies into this meal by making your crust out of cauliflower. Use my recipe in the Cauliflower Crust Pizza on page 127.

Cauliflower Crust Pizza
with Shaved Asparagus + Prosciutto

MAKES ONE 10- TO 12-INCH PIZZA

500↓ | FF | 50/50

My husband likes to eat low-carb, which is terrible! Yes, I know it's good for me, and yes, some-one like me who consumes carbs like a junkie could obviously use a break, but I just don't want to—especially when it comes to pizza! But what if there were a pizza that was big on flavor yet low on carbs? This is a game changer: Cauliflower Crust Pizza. There is plenty of cheese, it still warms your belly, it just doesn't add to it, and you can get as creative as you want with the top-pings. The crust uses cauliflower instead of flour; anytime a substitution like that works without sacrificing taste, I'm on board! In fact I'm the captain of that tasty ship!

Cauliflower Crust

1 small head cauliflower (about 1½ pounds),
    stems removed, coarsely chopped

1 cup shredded mozzarella cheese (4 ounces)

½ teaspoon dried oregano

¼ teaspoon garlic powder

¼ teaspoon kosher salt

1 large egg

Asparagus + Prosciutto Topping

5 asparagus stalks (about 3 ounces)

1 Fresno chile

8 ounces ricotta cheese

1 teaspoon minced fresh thyme leaves

Finely grated zest of ½ lemon

Kosher salt

1 to 2 slices prosciutto

Olive oil

Cauliflower Crust

1. Preheat the oven to 400°F.

2. Put the cauliflower in a food processor and pulse until finely ground. You may need to stir as you go to make sure the bigger pieces don't sit on the top. You should have about 4 cups.

3. Put the cauliflower in a large microwave-safe bowl and cook on high for 3 minutes, stir and cook for another 3 minutes. Drain any liquid that had collected in the bowl and let cool. When the cauliflower is cool enough to handle, transfer it to a kitchen towel or piece of cheesecloth; roll up the cloth and twist and squeeze out as much liquid as you can. Squeeze hard to get out all the excess water; this is crucial to getting a good crust. Once done you should have 1 to 1½ cups of dry cauliflower.

4. Line a baking sheet with parchment paper. Mix the cauliflower, mozzarella, oregano, garlic powder, and salt together. Add the egg and mix to combine; don't worry if the mixture seems too wet and loose. Transfer the cauliflower mixture to the baking sheet and shape it into a 10- to 12-inch-diameter round, about ¼–½ inch thick.

5. Bake the crust in the preheated oven until golden brown, about 20 minutes. While the crust bakes, prepare the Asparagus + Prosciutto Topping (below).

6. When the crust is done, remove the baking sheet from the oven, flip the crust, and increase the oven temperature to 475°F. Spread the ricotta topping mixture over the crust. Scatter the asparagus and chiles over the top and then sprinkle them with a little salt and add a drizzle of olive oil. Return the baking sheet to the oven and bake the pizza for 10 minutes. When it comes out of the oven, scatter the prosciutto over the top, cut into wedges, and serve.

Asparagus + Prosciutto Topping

Using a vegetable peeler, completely shave the asparagus spears into thin ribbons and put in a small bowl. Cut the chile crosswise into thin rounds. Stir together the ricotta, thyme, lemon zest, and ½ teaspoon salt in a second small bowl. Cut the prosciutto into ½-inch-wide strips.

FF

- This cauliflower crust will quickly become a staple in your home. Make the pie to completion except for the prosciutto, cool, and freeze. When you're ready to eat, bake the pie at 350°F for about 20 minutes until hot and crisp; top with the prosciutto and serve. Freeze the crusts with no topping, let thaw in the fridge, then top and bake as instructed above.
- The more you process the cauliflower the more it will look like a traditional crust.

50/50

With or without the prosciutto, this is a super-satisfying pie. But if you don't want one 50/50 pie, make 2 individual pizzas out of this recipe.

Oven-dried Tomatoes,
Pesto + Corn Pizza

Grilled Shiitake + Blueberry
Flatbread (p. 133)

Oven-dried Tomatoes, Pesto + Corn Pizza

MAKES TWO 9-INCH PIZZAS

50/50

Living in New York City, you learn to savor the summer months, eating outside with the sun on your shoulders, heatedly debating who really had the best tomato recently. This is summer! But what do you do the other nine months of the year? When fresh tomatoes are less than spectacular, I oven-dry them. By baking them until they shrivel up, you drastically intensify their sweetness and tomato flavor. In this recipe I cook them a bit hotter than normal and leave them a little juicy, creating an oven-dried tomato that bursts in your mouth and makes you feel like it's summer all over again. So dust off those sunglasses and get into the kitchen. It may be snowing outside, but it is summer in here.

5 plum tomatoes

¾ teaspoon kosher salt

¼ teaspoon ground black pepper

1 pound pizza dough, at room temperature

4 teaspoons olive oil

¼ cup Basil Pesto (page 163)

2 cups shredded mozzarella cheese (8 ounces)

1 cup frozen corn kernels

16 pepperoni slices

1. Preheat the oven to 400°F.

2. Cut the tomatoes into ½- to ¾-inch-thick rounds and toss them with the salt and pepper in a medium bowl. Place a wire rack on a rimmed baking sheet, spray or grease the wire rack and then arrange the tomatoes in a single layer on the rack. (If using an old rack spray or grease the rack first.) Roast in the oven until the tomatoes are shriveled and very slightly charred, 45 to 50 minutes. Remove the tomatoes from the oven and set aside. Increase the oven temperature to 500°F. Place a pizza stone or baking sheet in the oven to preheat.

3. Preheat a gas or charcoal grill (or plan to use a grill pan). Cut the pizza dough in half and roll out each piece on a lightly floured surface into a 9-inch-diameter round about ¼ inch thick. If using a grill pan,

place it over medium-high heat. Brush 1 teaspoon of the oil over each dough round; then grill it, oiled side down, until grill marks form and there are a few spots of medium brown on the bottom, about 3 minutes. (Grill one at a time if necessary). Brush 1 teaspoon of the oil over the top of each round and then flip the dough over and grill 3 minutes more. Set aside; the dough will not be fully cooked.

4. Spread half the pesto over each grilled crust. Then divide the mozzarella over each, followed by half the corn, half the tomatoes, and finally half the pepperoni. Open the oven and pull out the rack, then slide the pizza onto the hot stone or baking sheet. Push in the rack and bake the pizzas until cooked through and crisp and the pepperoni has curled up a bit, about 10 minutes. Cut each pizza in half and serve right away.

Keep It Simple

- Get a jump on this by roasting the tomatoes ahead of time. Refrigerate them in a food storage container for up to a week.
- You can always skip the grill or grill pan and simply top raw dough with the pesto, cheese, veggies, and pepperoni and bake these on a preheated pizza stone or baking sheet for 10 to 12 minutes. Assemble them on a rimless baking sheet or pizza peel that has been dusted with cornmeal so you can slide them onto the hot stone or preheated baking sheet (See Poblano + Ancho Cream Pizza for how to do).
- I like to finish this pizza in the oven because it gives me more control over the heat. But if you are a grill master, skip the oven and finish this pizza on your outdoor grill; just lower the temperature so that the crust doesn't overcook while the toppings bake.

50/50

You probably figured this out on your own: to please vegetarians, simply leave off the pepperoni from one or both pizzas.

Grilled Shiitake + Blueberry Flatbread

MAKES ONE 10 × 7-INCH FLATBREAD

Make It Meaty

I always love throwing fruit in places it doesn't normally belong. So I set out to make mushrooms and blueberries into something great. And with the addition of herbs, salty and chewy halloumi cheese, and spicy arugula, I believe I have done just that.

4 ounces halloumi cheese

3 tablespoons olive oil

7 ounces shiitake mushrooms, stems removed

2 garlic cloves, minced

2 teaspoons minced fresh thyme leaves

1 teaspoon minced fresh oregano leaves

½ cup fresh blueberries

8 ounces pizza dough, at room temperature

1 cup arugula

1. Pat the halloumi dry. Heat 1 teaspoon of the oil in a small nonstick skillet over medium-high heat. Add the cheese and sauté until golden on all sides—about 3 minutes per side. Cut it into bite-size pieces; set aside.

2. Preheat a gas or charcoal grill (or plan to use a grill pan). Chop the caps into bite-size pieces. Heat 2 tablespoons of the oil in a medium skillet over medium-low heat. Stir in the garlic and cook until fragrant, 2 to 3 minutes. Increase the heat to high; stir in the mushrooms, and cook until they are tender and slightly brown, 5 to 7 minutes more. Add the thyme and oregano, and cook for 2 minutes. Remove the skillet from the heat and stir in the blueberries and cheese. Cover and keep warm.

3. Roll out the dough on a lightly floured surface into an oval or to fit your grill or grill pan about ¼ inch thick. If using a grill pan, place it over medium heat. Brush the remaining 1 teaspoon oil over the dough; then grill it, oiled side down, until brown on the bottom, 5 minutes. Brush the remaining 1 teaspoon oil over the top of the dough, flip it over and brown the other side, about 5 minutes more.

4. Transfer the crust to a cutting board. Spread the mushroom mixture over it, leaving a 1-inch border all around. Scatter the arugula over the top. Cut the flatbread into wedges and serve hot or at room temperature.

Fennel + Red Onion Jam Puff Pizza

MAKES ONE 11½-INCH-SQUARE PIZZA

500↓ | Make It Meaty

Puff pastry is one of those things you don't have to feel guilty about buying at the grocery store. It is made by folding butter into dough many times until you have endless layers of the two; when cooked it puffs up as the butter melts and steams. It's a dough that takes far too much time and technique to make yourself and is better left to the professionals. So I pick up a package of puff pastry sheets and create all sorts of dishes with this store-bought gem. For this pizza it creates a delicate and rich crust that is flaky and sweet. Topped with fennel, red onion jam, bacon, and hot peppers, it's an elegant pizza that takes just minutes to prep.

1 small fennel bulb (about 4 ounces), trimmed and very thinly sliced

½ cup coarsely chopped, cored, and seeded red bell pepper

1 Thai or cayenne chile, seeded and minced

1 tablespoon olive oil

½ teaspoon kosher salt

Finely grated zest of ½ lemon

2 bacon strips

One 10-inch-square sheet frozen puff pastry, thawed

½ cup Red Onion Jam (page 225)

1 cup shredded mozzarella cheese (4 ounces)

Fresh thyme leaves, for garnish

1. Preheat the oven to 400°F. Line a baking sheet with parchment paper.

2. Toss the fennel, bell peppers, and chiles with the oil, salt, and lemon zest in a large bowl.

3. Preheat a small skillet over medium-low heat. Add the bacon and cook for 3 minutes, turning once; you don't want it to be completely crispy as it will finish cooking in the oven. Transfer the bacon to a paper towel to drain; then chop it into very small pieces.

4. When the oven is hot, place the pastry on a lightly floured surface and roll it out to a 12-inch square. Transfer the pastry to the prepared baking sheet. Roll up ¼ inch of the pastry on each edge to form a bit of a rim and then prick the pastry all over with a fork. Spread the jam over the pastry leaving the rim bare. Scatter the mozzarella evenly over the jam and then scatter the fennel mixture and bacon over the top. Bake the pizza until the crust is puffy and golden brown and the cheese has melted, 25 to 30 minutes. Sprinkle with the thyme and then cut into quarters or rectangles. Enjoy hot!

Keep It Simple

• If your timing is off, put the thawed pastry in the refrigerator until you are ready to use it. Puff pastry should always stay as cold as possible (but not frozen) until it goes in the oven.

• The Red Onion Jam recipe makes quite a bit more than you need for this pizza. You can freeze the extra or refrigerate it and use it over the next couple days as a condiment on your sandwich, as a topping for fish or chicken, or simply as a spread on toast.

• Instead of my homemade Red Onion Jam, spread ¼ cup of your favorite jam on the pastry (I like raspberry or apricot); then chop half a small red onion and add it to the fennel and pepper mixture. A nice squeeze of lemon juice is good on this version, too.

• You can substitute ¼ teaspoon crushed red pepper flakes for the hot pepper.

Make It Meaty

The crust of this pizza is more delicate than a normal pizza crust, so you don't want to load up on the toppings. However, some nice cooked chicken can be great. Finely chop or shred 3 ounces of chicken and place it right on the jam, under the cheese so it stays nice and moist.

PIZZA PEEL?! YES!

Tears are not often shed in my kitchen, but the event has taken place. It actually became a frequent occurrence years ago when I really got on a pizza-making kick. I had acquired the ESSENTIAL pizza-making tool: the pizza stone. This magical stone cooks the bottom of the crust to crisp perfection as it wicks away moisture, keeping the center chewy. The stone changed my pizza-making experience. There was only one problem: transferring the perfectly topped raw pizza onto the stone that had been preheated in the oven. And this is where the tears came in . . .

There is nothing sadder than making a homemade sauce, spreading it on your perfectly tossed dough, topping it with the best of ingredients and then in the final step completely ruining it trying to transfer it to the hot pizza stone. My husband would console me as we ate deformed, inside-out, raw-on-one-side/cooked-on-the-other pizzas.

So, though I do not have the space for it, I finally acquired a pizza peel, just like John and Mike at my favorite NYC pizzeria! Now I am a pizza-producing machine, and most important, there are no more tears.

Summer Squash

Summer squash come in many shapes, sizes, and colors, but all are very similar in flavor and can be substituted for each other in recipes. Unlike winter squash, these guys are best harvested when they are young and their skins are delicate, meaning you can eat the skin, flesh, and seeds. And you definitely want to eat the skin as it is where many of the antioxidants in the squash live. But what do you do when you've planted them in your garden and suddenly have a harvest of 20 green and yellow squash staring at you? You make pasta and crostini out of it, stuff it in quiches, roll it around cheese, and of course top your bagel with it (trust me!). So whether your garden is exploding with them or they are crazy cheap at the store this summer, you are hereby well prepared to take on summer squash.

Recipe List

Eggplant

Eggplant's meaty taste means that you can use it in place of beef, pork, or chicken to create dishes that are vegetarian—or nearly so—yet still deeply, intensely flavorful. And its unique texture means you can puree this purple fruit (yes, fruit!) and transform it into sauces and even "meatballs." After you start to look at an eggplant the way I do, you will be finding it constantly on your plate. And that's good for your brain and heart as well as your stomach. The antioxidants in eggplant help protect brain cells while also improving cholesterol levels, all while its fiber leaves you satisfied and full, making this purple guy, pretty darn special.

Recipe List

Zucchini Crust Pizza

MAKES FOUR 5-INCH PIZZAS

500↓ | FF | Make It Meaty

When you make the crust of a pizza mostly out of veggies you can always feel really good about your meal. The first time I made cauliflower into a crust I knew there were other vegetables that needed to join the veggie-crust party. Zucchini was an easy choice with its mild flavor and delicate texture. And as soon as I'd decided that, fresh tomatoes, milky mozzarella, and my Garden-Fresh Tomato Sauce seemed like obvious choices to put on top, all creating a pie you feel so good about eating that you can have two. ;)

Zucchini Crust

3 medium zucchini (about 2 pounds)

¾ cup grated Pecorino Romano cheese (3 ounces)

½ cup all-purpose flour

1 large egg

Topping

1 cup Garden-Fresh Tomato Sauce (page 222)

8 ounces fresh mozzarella, cut into strips

12 cherry or grape tomatoes, halved (a mix of red and yellow is nice!)

¼ cup finely chopped fresh basil leaves

Zucchini Crust

1. Preheat the oven to 400°F. Line a baking sheet with parchment paper.

2. Grate the zucchini with a box grater or the shredder attachment on a food processor; you should have about 6 cups. Put the zucchini in a large microwave-safe bowl and microwave on high until it is tender and the liquid has collected in the bottom of the bowl, about 7 minutes, stirring after 3½ minutes.

3. Set the zucchini aside until it is cool enough to handle. Then, using a slotted spoon, or your hands, transfer it to a clean kitchen towel or piece of cheesecloth. Roll up the cloth, and twist and squeeze out as much liquid as you can—squeeze hard to get out all the excess water—this is crucial to getting a good crust. You should end up with about 2 cups cooked shredded zucchini.

4. Add the zucchini, Pecorino Romano, flour, and egg to a medium bowl and stir until blended into a dough. Divide the dough into 4 equal pieces. Shape each into a ball and place it on the prepared baking sheet, spacing the balls at least 6 inches apart. Using your hands, flatten each ball of dough into a 5-inch-diameter round, ¼ to ½ inch thick. Place the baking sheet in the oven and bake the crusts until golden brown and firm, about 20 minutes. Remove the baking sheet from the oven, but leave the oven on.

Topping

Flip each crust over on the baking sheet. Spread one-quarter of the tomato sauce over each and top with one-quarter of the mozzarella strips. Return the baking sheet to the oven and bake until the cheese has melted and slightly browned, 20 to 25 minutes. Top each pizza with 6 cherry tomato halves and sprinkle it with 1 tablespoon of the chopped basil. Serve and enjoy!

FF

- These are great for kids!! They will love the gooey cheese and pepperonis, and you will love the 6 cups of veggies in the crust. Pecorino Romano cheese can be a little strong, so if you want to tone it down, use a nice Parmesan or even shredded mozzarella for a very mild flavor. And, of course, feel free to top these pizzas with whatever toppings your family loves.
- You can wrap these cooked pizzas individually, and freeze them. You'll have single serving, gourmet frozen pizzas ready for any meal.

Make It Meaty

For a meatier pie add 3–4 slices of pepperoni onto each along with the mozzarella. Cooked and crumbled sausage is also nice.

Pasta + "Pasta"

Colorful Cauliflower + Scallop Pasta
with Brown Butter + Herbs

MAKES 4 SERVINGS

FF | 50/50

Instead of a bar, I'm a regular at my farmers' market. And in the fall, when I come across cauliflower in a rainbow of colors, you know I'm adding it to my already ridiculously overstuffed bag. Because then I can make this simple and simply special pasta: Browned butter, fragrant garlic, bright lemon, and tender scallops, add some purple, orange, and green cauliflower and you just may have to take a picture before you dig in, it's that pretty. Luckily, the flavor of these cauliflowers is the same as the white stuff, so even in the dead of winter, when no market sports the colorful types, you can still snuggle up with a bowl of this pasta while binge-watching *Junk Food Flip* and have the most perfect evening ever.

8 tablespoons (1 stick) unsalted butter

1 medium yellow onion, finely chopped

1 pound linguine

6 cups different color cauliflower florets (from 2 small or 1 large head)

1 small head purple cauliflower, broken into small florets

3 garlic cloves, sliced

2½ teaspoons kosher salt

½ cup white wine or chicken stock

¼ cup chopped mixed fresh herbs, such as parsley, thyme, and oregano, plus more for garnish

Finely grated zest and juice of 1 lemon

1 tablespoon olive oil

1 pound bay scallops

1. Place a large pot of salted water over high heat for cooking the linguine. Melt the butter in a large saucepan over medium heat and then cook it until browned, about 5 minutes. Stir in the onion and cook for 3 minutes.

2. When the water boils, add the linguine and cook according to the package directions until al dente. Drain, reserving 2 cups of the cooking water.

3. Meanwhile, add the cauliflower, garlic, and 2 teaspoons of the salt to the pan with the onion and cook until the garlic is fragrant and the cauliflower is tender, about 7 minutes. Add the wine and cook until it has been absorbed by the cauliflower, 3 to 4 minutes.

4. Add the linguine to the pan with the cauliflower and stir in the herbs, lemon zest, lemon juice, and enough of the reserved pasta cooking water to achieve a saucy consistency. Keep warm on low heat while you cook the scallops.

5. Heat the oil in a large skillet over high heat, add the scallops, sprinkle them with the remaining ½ teaspoon salt, and cook for 1 minute. Flip and cook 30 seconds on the opposite side. Add the scallops to the pasta and toss to combine, adding more of the cooking water if needed. Serve garnished with extra herbs if desired.

Keep It Simple

Bay scallops can vary in price, but will always be cheapest if you can find them locally in the summer. If you're looking for a cheaper off-season option, or want to try something different, chopped cooked chicken breast, shrimp (rock to jumbo), and my Eggplant Meatballs (page 196) are all nice options.

FF

You can make the cauliflower "disappear" and look like cheese on the pasta: In step 3, use chicken stock or even water instead of wine. Then put the cooked cauliflower in a food processor and pulse to a couscouslike consistency. Return it to the pan and complete the recipe as written.

50/50

This pasta is great with or without the scallops. For every vegetarian portion you want, omit ¼ pound of the scallops; then add the scallops to the pasta once it is on the individual plates instead of tossing everything together in the pan.

Brussels Sprouts + Pear Carbonara

MAKES 4 ENTRÉE PORTIONS

10-in-30 | FF | 50 /50

Brussels sprouts didn't make a regular appearance in my meals until quite recently. At first their bitterness was an unwanted one, but what I have found is that the key to balancing out these bitter little nuggets is to add something a tad sweet—like pears, for instance. Combine that with a little bacon (or not) and a rich, eggy carbonara sauce, and you bring out the best in this shrunken cabbage. Its bitterness perfectly cuts through the richness of the pasta sauce while the pear adds that wanted touch of sweetness. You'll be making your inner child shudder as you greedily go back for another perfect bite of pear, pasta, and of course Brussels sprouts!

1 pound Brussels sprouts

2 tablespoons olive oil

3 teaspoons kosher salt

1 pound linguine

4 bacon strips, chopped into ½- to 1-inch pieces

3 shallots, finely chopped

3 garlic cloves, minced

4 large egg yolks, at room temperature

¼ cup heavy cream, at room temperature

1 cup grated Parmesan cheese (4 ounces)

2 pears, peeled, cored, and finely chopped

½ cup thinly sliced scallions

1. Preheat the oven to 475°F.

2. Cut the Brussels sprouts into quarters and put in a medium bowl. Add the oil and 1 teaspoon of the salt and toss to coat. Spread the sprouts out evenly on a rimmed baking sheet.

3. Bring a large pot of salted water to a boil over high heat. Place the Brussels sprouts in the oven and roast until they are tender and charred, 20 to 25 minutes. As soon as the water boils, cook the pasta according to the package directions until al dente. Drain the pasta, reserving 2 cups of the cooking water.

4. Meanwhile, heat a large skillet over medium heat. Add the bacon and cook until crisp, 6 to 7 minutes, stirring occasionally. Transfer the bacon to paper towels to drain, leaving the fat in the skillet. Add the shallots and garlic to the skillet and sauté until soft, about 5 minutes. Stir in the pasta and remove the skillet from the heat.

5. Whisk together the egg yolks and cream in a small bowl. Slowly add ½ cup of the reserved pasta cooking water to the egg mixture, whisking as you go; you don't want to cook the eggs, so add the hot water very slowly. Add the egg mixture to the pan with the pasta and stir vigorously until well incorporated. Place the skillet over low heat and add the Parmesan and the remaining 2 teaspoons salt and toss to combine. Finally add the Brussels sprouts, pears, and bacon and stir gently until distributed through the pasta. Gradually stir in as much as you need of the remaining pasta cooking water to give the mixture a saucy consistency. Serve immediately, with the scallions scattered on top of each portion.

FF

- For a sweeter taste overall, use the outer leaves of the Brussels sprouts only and chop them small; they are less bitter than the center.
- As soon as the Brussels sprouts are out of the oven, sprinkle with a little Parmesan to make them look and taste a bit more appetizing for picky eaters. You can also cook them for only 15 minutes to achieve a less charred flavor.
- Sometimes dinners have to wait on the stovetop while everyone gathers. Keep extra pasta water on hand and add it as needed to keep the pasta nice and saucy. It will be ready when you are.

50/50

- For a completely vegetarian meal, simply leave out the bacon and sauté the shallots and garlic in 1 tablespoon olive oil.
- To make this dish for a mixed household (vegetarians and meat eaters alike) sauté the bacon (1 piece per person) and set aside in the pan. Complete the recipe as written, but sauté the shallots and garlic in 1 tablespoon of olive oil in a second large skillet. Serve the pasta, adding some bacon and a drizzle of its fat to each meat-eater's portion.

Linguine + Red Pepper Clam Sauce

MAKES 4 SERVINGS

50/50

I love peppers; in fact my husband calls me the female Bobby Flay. And since I am not a six-foot-tall male with red hair, I assume he is saying it because of my love for peppers—big, small, sweet, and spicy ones. I think the role of a pepper can be exponentially more special than as a mere tool for dipping up ranch dressing on a crudité platter, and in this recipe I prove it. The sauce is complex, spicy, sweet, and smoky, and the addition of clams gives the whole dish another layer of briny flavor that takes its turn at waking up your taste buds. This dish is exploding with flavor. That's the power of peppers.

3 red bell peppers

1 jalapeño chile

2 scallions, chopped

3 garlic cloves

1 tablespoon fresh thyme leaves

1 tablespoon fresh mint leaves

1 teaspoon kosher salt

1 teaspoon paprika

4 tablespoons unsalted butter

1 pound linguine

3 pounds littleneck clams, scrubbed clean

1½ cups clam juice (bottled is fine)

1 lemon, quartered lengthwise

1. Use the broiler or a gas burner on the stovetop to roast the bell peppers and jalapeño: Simply place them under the heat source or over the flame (use tongs if you're working on the stovetop) and cook until they are mostly black on all sides, 2 to 3 minutes for the jalapeño, 5 to 8 minutes for the bell peppers, turning as needed. Put the jalapeño and peppers in a plastic food storage bag and seal the bag. When they have cooled, rub off the skins with paper towels. Cut the jalapeño open lengthwise and remove its stem and seeds. Quarter the bell peppers lengthwise and remove their stem and seeds.

2. Place a large pot of salted water over high heat for cooking the pasta. While it is heating, add the red peppers, jalapeño, scallions, garlic, thyme, mint, salt, and paprika to a food processor. Pulse until finely

chopped; you want this mixture to be almost pureed. Melt the butter in a large saucepan over medium-high heat. Stir in the red pepper mixture and cook, stirring frequently, until the garlic and scallions become tender and fragrant, 3 to 5 minutes.

3. Add the linguine to the now-boiling water and cook until just shy of al dente—a little less time than indicated on the package. Drain the pasta.

4. Meanwhile, add the clams and clam juice to the red pepper sauce. Stir, cover, and cook until all the clams have opened up, 6 to 8 minutes.

5. Add the linguine to the pepper and clam sauce and toss until well combined. Reduce the heat to low and cook for 2 to 3 minutes; this allows the linguine to finish cooking and the flavors to come together. Serve the pasta immediately, passing the lemon quarters at the table so that each diner can squeeze some juice over their own serving.

Keep It Simple

Get a jump on this with jarred roasted red peppers. If you do, you can throw the jalapeño in raw—roasted is nice, but not essential.

50/50

- To make half the portions vegetarian, use only 1½ pounds of clams and cook them in a separate pot with ¾ cup clam juice, letting them steam until open. Toss half the pasta and sauce in that pot. Then, to add a little zip to the remaining vegetarian portions, stir 1 tablespoon red wine vinegar into the sauce and heat briefly before adding the pasta. For the vegetarian version reserve some of the pasta's cooking liquid to thin the sauce on these portions as you like.
- If you want to omit the clams entirely, add 2 tablespoons of red wine vinegar in step 2 along with 1 cup of the pasta's cooking liquid.

Fire Island Burst-Tomato Pasta

MAKES 4 SERVINGS

FF | 50/50

I vividly remember how intense and overwhelming it was being on *Food Network Star,* but even knowing that I would do it all over again. Though I definitely treasured the experience I also missed my normal life. So, when given the opportunity to make a pasta dish on the show, I knew I had to make this one, as it reminded me of making seaside dinners with my inspiring father-in-law Bob's tomatoes right off the vine. And to my surprise, this dish that I made mostly for sentimental reasons became the most popular recipe from the entire show.

Burst-Tomato Pasta

4 ounces soft goat cheese

1 tablespoon finely chopped fresh flat-leaf parsley

Finely grated zest of 1 lemon

¼ cup extra-virgin olive oil

8 garlic cloves, sliced

6 to 8 large tomatoes, cut into 1-inch chunks, or 3 pints cherry or grape tomatoes

3 to 4 tablespoons chopped fresh basil leaves, plus hand-torn leaves for garnish

2 teaspoons kosher salt, plus more as needed

1 teaspoon red wine vinegar

1 pound linguine

Breaded Chicken

4 chicken cutlets

½ cup all-purpose flour

1½ teaspoons kosher salt

⅛ teaspoon ground black pepper

1 large egg

1 tablespoon water

2 cups dry plain bread crumbs

Burst-Tomato Pasta

1. Mix together the goat cheese, parsley, and lemon zest in a small bowl. Using your hands, roll the mixture into small balls. Put the balls in a bowl, cover, and refrigerate.

2. Place a large pot of salted water over high heat for cooking the pasta. While it is heating, heat the oil in a large saucepan over medium-low heat. Stir in the garlic and cook until fragrant and tender but not browned, 5 to 7 minutes.

3. Add the tomatoes to the pan with the garlic and cook until tender, 15 to 20 minutes. While the tomatoes cook, prep the Breaded Chicken (below) through step 2.

4. Smash down the tomatoes with a wooden spoon and stir in 3 tablespoons of the basil and the salt and vinegar. Continue to cook until the sauce reaches a consistency you like, 5 to 15 minutes. (My preference is sauce that's not too wet but still able to coat the pasta.) Reduce the heat to low to keep the sauce warm. Meanwhile, while the sauce cooks, add the linguine to the now-boiling water and cook according to the package directions until al dente. Also complete step 3 of the Breaded Chicken.

5. When the linguine is done, drain it, reserving 1 cup of the cooking water. Taste the sauce and add more salt or chopped basil if you wish. Add the linguine to the sauce and toss to mix. If your sauce is thicker than you like, stir in some of the cooking water to thin it.

6. To serve, divide the sauced linguine among four dinner plates. Arrange the chicken on top of each portion. Drop a few of the herbed cheese balls on top and scatter some torn basil over all.

Breaded Chicken

1. Preheat the oven to 450°F. Whisk together the flour, ¼ teaspoon of the salt, and ⅛ teaspoon of the pepper on a small plate. Whisk together the egg, water, ¼ teaspoon of the salt, and ⅛ teaspoon of the pepper in a shallow bowl. Mix the bread crumbs with the remaining 1 teaspoon salt and ¼ teaspoon pepper in a second shallow bowl.

2. One at a time, dip each cutlet first in the flour, turning to dust each side and shaking off any excess; then into the egg mixture, turning to coat both sides and allowing any excess to drip off; and finally into the bread crumbs, making sure the crumbs coat all sides of the cutlet. Lay the coated cutlets on a wire rack set on a baking sheet. You can drizzle or spray the cutlets with olive oil if you like but it's not necessary.

3. Bake the chicken until it is cooked through, 8 to 10 minutes. Let the cutlets rest for 2 to 3 minutes, then cut them crosswise into 1-inch-wide strips.

FF

- Up the nutritional value of this dish by replacing the pasta with zucchini noodles, and at the same time, get your family hooked on a veggie they may not already love. (See Zucchini Noodles on page 166.)
- You can also puree the sauce.

50/50

Simply omit the chicken from each portion you wish to make vegetarian. This sauce is flavorful and hearty enough to enjoy without the meat.

Pumpkin-Poblano Pasta
with Baby Bok Choy + Shrimp

MAKES 4 SERVINGS

FF | 50/50

A fan of mine recently asked me to help him develop a meal for the night he was going to propose to his girlfriend. I was a total sucker for the idea and took all of her favorite things, including her beloved pumpkin lattes, and wrapped them up into this dish. If she doesn't want to marry him, I've got about ten friends who would jump at the chance . . . assuming he comes with this meal in hand of course.

1 poblano chile

3 tablespoons olive oil

2 shallots, coarsely chopped

4 garlic cloves, minced

1 teaspoon minced fresh thyme leaves

1½ teaspoons kosher salt

One 15-ounce can 100 percent pure pumpkin puree

3 ounces soft goat cheese, crumbled

Pinch of ground nutmeg

Pinch of ground cinnamon

1 pound bucatini

4 baby bok choys, chopped into 1-inch pieces

16 jumbo shrimp (16/20), peeled and deveined

¼ cup chopped scallions, green parts only

¼ cup roasted pumpkin seeds (see Appendix, page 261)

1. Use the broiler or a gas burner on the stovetop to roast the poblano: Simply place it under the heat source or over the flame (use tongs if you're working on the stovetop) and cook until mostly black on all sides, 5 to 8 minutes, turning as needed. Put the poblano in a plastic food storage bag and seal the bag. When the poblano has cooled, rub off the skin with a paper towel. Cut the poblano open lengthwise and remove its stem and seeds.

2. Place a large pot of salted water over high heat for cooking the pasta. While it is heating, heat 2 tablespoons of the oil in a large skillet over medium heat. Stir in the shallots and garlic and sauté until tender, about 5 minutes. Stir in the thyme and 1 teaspoon of the salt until incorporated, then stir in the pumpkin, mix well, and cook for 3 minutes more.

3. Transfer the pumpkin mixture to a food processor or blender. Add the poblano and process to a smooth puree. Spoon the mixture back into the skillet. Stir in about two-thirds of the cheese along with the nutmeg and cinnamon; you'll use the rest of the cheese for garnish. Keep the skillet over low heat while you prepare the rest of the dish.

4. Cook the pasta in the now-boiling water according to the package directions until al dente. Drain the pasta, reserving 1 cup of the cooking water.

5. While the pasta is cooking, heat the remaining 1 tablespoon oil in a second large skillet over medium heat. Stir in the bok choy, sprinkle with ¼ teaspoon of the salt, and cook until tender, 3 to 5 minutes, stirring occasionally. Transfer the bok choy to a medium bowl. Add the shrimp to the same skillet, sprinkle with the remaining ¼ teaspoon salt, and sauté until pink, about 5 minutes, turning once. Return the bok choy to the skillet and heat through.

6. Add the drained pasta to the skillet with the pumpkin sauce and toss to coat. If the sauce seems too thick, stir in some of the reserved pasta cooking water to achieve your desired consistency.

7. Serve immediately, dividing the pasta equally among four dinner plates, and top each portion with one-quarter of the bok choy and 4 shrimp. Scatter the scallions, pumpkin seeds, and remaining cheese evenly over the tops.

Keep It Simple

- Substitute kale, radicchio, or cabbage for the bok choy.
- Use 2 to 3 tablespoons of heavy cream instead of the goat cheese. Also add a sprinkle of Parmesan to bump up the flavor if you have it on hand.
- If you don't want to bother with roasting the poblano chile, simply seed and chop it, and puree with the pumpkin in step 3: a quick alternative for a similar taste.
- If you can't find poblanos substitute a green pepper and add a sprinkle of cayenne or chili powder to the pumpkin mixture.

FF

Leave out the bok choy for pickier eaters, or cut it up very finely and add it to the pumpkin poblano mixture and they will never know it's in there.

50/50

This pasta is as good without shrimp as it is with; simply omit the shrimp to give vegetarians a satisfying meal. If you're making some veggie versions and some shrimp ones, just cook the shrimp separately and add to the plates you want.

Eggplant Sauce

MAKES 4 CUPS SAUCE

500↓ | FF

I like a lot of "bang for my bite" when it comes to my food. I love delicious meals that also pack a nutritional punch. And when you puree two giant eggplants along with peppers and tomatoes to make your sauce you get just that. This sauce almost reminds you of tomato sauce, but it has a subtly unique flavor. And the eggplant creates a super smooth base that brings all the flavors together. Looks like it's time to shake up pasta night.

2 red bell peppers	¼ cup red wine vinegar
2 extra-large eggplants (about 3 pounds total)	½ cup lightly packed fresh basil leaves
2 tablespoons olive oil	4 garlic cloves
One 16-ounce can tomato sauce	1 tablespoon kosher salt, plus more as needed

1. Use the broiler or a gas burner on the stovetop to roast the peppers: Simply place them under the heat source or over the flame (use tongs if you're working on the stovetop) and cook until they are mostly black on all sides, 5 to 8 minutes, turning as needed. Put the peppers in a plastic food storage bag and seal the bag. When the peppers have cooled, rub off the skins with a paper towel. Quarter the peppers lengthwise and then remove their stems and seeds.

2. Preheat the oven to 450°F.

3. Cut the eggplants in half lengthwise and place them, cut side up, on a rimmed baking sheet. Drizzle with the oil. When the oven is hot, bake the eggplants until the sides are soft to the touch, 25 to 30 minutes. Transfer the baking sheet to a wire rack. When the eggplants are cool enough to handle, use a spoon to scrape the flesh into a food processor or blender; discard the skins.

4. Add the tomato sauce, peppers, vinegar, basil, garlic, and salt to the food processor. Process until the sauce is smooth and well combined.

5. Transfer the sauce to a medium saucepan and simmer over medium heat until the garlic is less pungent, 5 to 7 minutes. Taste the sauce and add more salt if needed. Cover and keep the sauce warm over low heat until ready to add to your recipe.

Keep It Simple

Make this Eggplant Sauce ahead of time and refrigerate or freeze it until you need it (it will keep in the fridge up to 5 days, or in the freezer up to 2 months). I use it in my Tomato Parm, too (page 249), so I store it in 1- or 2-cup quantities and then I'm set to go for a variety of uses. Though I prefer using roasted peppers you can always saute up the peppers instead of roasting them and then add them to the food processor with the eggplant. Store-bought roasted peppers in a jar work great also.

FF

Nervous about kids and EGGPLANT sauce? Make the introduction by serving it with the type of pasta your kids normally eat: elbows, penne, whatever they like works.

Eggplant Pasta Bake
with Fresh Mozzarella
+ Thyme Bread Crumbs

MAKES 4 SERVINGS

Make It Meaty | FF

Tomato sauce was always on the list of "Nikki-Friendly Foods," as long as it wasn't too chunky of course. So what I love about this pasta bake recipe is that the Eggplant Sauce tastes like a cousin to tomato sauce; it's familiar tasting while taking the flavor you are used to up a notch. And when it's paired with good pasta and chunks of milky mozzarella and topped with crunchy bread crumbs, it creates a casserole that is really out of this world. Making this a dish that is "everyone friendly."

1 pound shell pasta

3 cups homemade coarse bread crumbs (see Appendix, page 259)

1 heaping tablespoon minced fresh thyme leaves

1 teaspoon kosher salt

3 tablespoons melted unsalted butter

4 cups Eggplant Sauce, warmed (page 158)

1 pound fresh mozzarella, cut into ½-inch cubes

1 pint cherry tomatoes, halved

1. Bring a large pot of salted water to the boil. Add the pasta and cook according to the package directions until al dente. While it cooks, combine the bread crumbs, thyme, and salt in a medium bowl, add the butter, and toss until the crumbs are evenly coated.

2. When the pasta is done, drain it and return it to the pot. Add the Eggplant Sauce, mozzarella, and cherry tomatoes and stir until the cheese begins to melt and the tomatoes warm through. (If the mixture isn't hot enough to melt the cheese, put the pot over medium heat for a few minutes and keep stirring until it is.)

3. Turn on the broiler. Spoon the pasta mixture into a 9 × 13-inch baking dish. Sprinkle the bread crumb mixture evenly over the top. Broil until the topping is crisp and slightly brown, 3 to 5 minutes. Serve immediately.

Keep It Simple

I like the chunks of mozzarella swimming throughout the dish, but if you only have shredded mozzarella on hand you can use that by sprinkling it between the pasta and bread crumbs for a great cheesy layer.

FF

The Eggplant Sauce is so smooth and it tastes just slightly different from tomato sauce, so this bake should go over as well as any pasta suppers you might normally serve. Using shredded mozzarella instead of fresh will ensure a very cheesy bite and an irresistible looking plate of pasta for your young ones.

Make It Meaty

A great addition to this dish is cooked, crumbled sausage. I like to use a hot Italian sausage. Cook up the sausage in a skillet, place it atop the pasta, top everything with the bread crumbs, and cook as instructed. You'll need three 3- to 4-ounce sausage links for this recipe. Or make it 50/50 and just put the sausage on half!

Parsnip Noodles + Basil Pesto

MAKES 4 SERVINGS; ABOUT 1½ CUPS PESTO

10-in-30 | Make It Meaty

I love my noodles, from pasta to ramen to soba: If we are talking comfort food, to me, we are talking noodles. And I am always on the lookout for an alternative noodle to balance out the excessive carbs that tend to find their way onto my plate. While zucchini noodles are great (see page 166) I knew there had to be something else. So, after much experimentation, may I present—parsnip noodles!! They are pliable and soft when cooked while retaining a bit of texture; they are the color of pasta and can be made into "noodles" with just a vegetable peeler; no fancy equipment required. Nothing makes me happier than noodles that you can feel really good about eating. Seconds anyone?!

Basil Pesto

3 cups packed fresh basil leaves

¼ cup pine nuts

4 garlic cloves

¾ cup grated Parmesan cheese (3 ounces)

¼ to ½ cup extra-virgin olive oil

¼ to ½ teaspoon salt, if needed

Parsnip Noodles

1 pint grape or cherry tomatoes, halved

1¼ teaspoons kosher salt

6 large parsnips (about 2 pounds)

1 tablespoon extra-virgin olive oil

Basil Pesto

Put the basil, pine nuts, garlic, and Parmesan in a food processor or blender and process until finely chopped. With the machine running, slowly add ¼ cup of the olive oil through the feed tube; add up to another ¼ cup as needed—you want the pesto to be loose and pourable. Taste the pesto to see if it needs salt; this will depend on how salty the cheese is. If it does, add ¼ to ½ teaspoon, tasting again as you go. Set aside.

Parsnip Noodles

1. Toss the tomatoes in a medium bowl with ¼ teaspoon of the salt.

2. Using a vegetable peeler, remove and discard the skin from the parsnips. Shave each parsnip into strips, turning it frequently as you go to keep the strips narrow like fettuccine.

3. Briefly heat the oil in a large skillet over medium heat. Add the parsnips, sprinkle with the remaining 1 teaspoon salt, and cook until soft but not mushy, 5 to 7 minutes, tossing with tongs occasionally.

4. Add half of the pesto to the parsnips in the skillet and toss with the tongs to mix. Reduce the heat to low and add more pesto until all the parsnips are coated and you have the amount of sauce that you like; cook for 2 to 3 minutes more.

5. To serve, divide the parsnip noodles equally among four plates and top each serving with one-quarter of the tomatoes. Enjoy!

Keep It Simple

The look will not be as pastalike, but you can substitute carrots for the parsnips for a similar taste and texture.

Make It Meaty

Breaded Chicken (see page 154) and Tiny Chicken Meatballs (page 223) are both fantastic with this "pasta." You can also go in a seafood direction and serve with cod, tilapia, or shrimp. Eggplant "Meat-balls" (page 196) are great, too, but not truly meaty.

Zucchini Noodles + Apricot-Glazed Pork

MAKES 4 SERVINGS

500↓ | 50/50

Who doesn't love birthdays? For me, growing up with four siblings, it was the one day I could force my entire family to eat "Picky Nikki" cuisine. Though I was on cloud nine, it was obvious no one else thought my meal of plain lasagna noodles, ramen, and Italian bread was as delicious as I did. For me, carbs were exactly what made that meal special. They still play a starring role in my dinners today, but I'm always looking for interesting ways to swap them for more nutritious veggies. Here I've replaced regular noodles with zucchini and bean sprouts, and, as a certified carb-expert (yes, I've made myself a badge), I can vouch that you really don't miss them.

Apricot-Glazed Pork

1½ cups apricot juice

1 tablespoon sugar

2 teaspoons rice wine vinegar

1 teaspoon cornstarch

1 tablespoon water

1 tablespoon olive oil

1 pound pork tenderloin, cut into 1-inch pieces

1 teaspoon kosher salt

Zucchini Noodles

5 large zucchini (about 3½ pounds total)

1 teaspoon sesame oil

1 tablespoon vegetable oil or olive oil

4 scallions, white and green parts chopped
    separately

1 teaspoon peeled and grated fresh ginger

3 garlic cloves, minced

1½ cups coarsely chopped broccoli florets

1½ cups sliced mini orange bell peppers

¼ cup soy sauce

1 tablespoon mirin

1 tablespoon sriracha sauce

1 tablespoon rice wine vinegar

3 cups bean sprouts

4 radishes, very thinly sliced

Apricot-Glazed Pork

1. Pour the apricot juice into a small pan over medium heat. Let it simmer until it has reduced by half and thickened, 20 minutes. Stir in the sugar and vinegar and continue to simmer until the syrup has reduced to about ⅓ cup.

2. Combine the cornstarch with the water in a small bowl and whisk until dissolved. Whisk the slurry mixture into the syrup and simmer until the syrup is thick enough to coat the back of a spoon, 2 minutes more. Remove from the heat.

3. Heat the oil in a medium skillet over high heat. Sprinkle the salt evenly over the pork. Add the pork to the skillet and sauté until seared on all sides, 3 to 5 minutes total. Stir the syrup into the skillet, mixing to coat the pork. Cover and keep warm.

Zucchini Noodles

1. Cut the zucchini into spaghetti-size noodles; use a mandoline fitted with a julienne attachment, a julienne peeler, or a spiralizer. Or simply use a regular vegetable peeler, which will give you pappardelle-style noodles.

2. Heat the sesame and vegetable oils in a large deep skillet over high heat. Stir in the scallion whites, ginger, and garlic and cook until fragrant, 2 to 3 minutes. Stir in the broccoli and peppers and cook until crisp-tender, 3 to 5 minutes. Add the soy sauce, mirin, sriracha, and vinegar and toss everything together, mixing well.

3. Add the zucchini and bean sprouts to the vegetable mixture and stir to distribute evenly. Cook until crisp-tender, 5 minutes more. Serve immediately, dividing the zucchini mixture equally among four bowls and topping each with one-quarter of the pork, scallion greens, and radishes.

Keep It Simple

- Julienne the zucchini, chop the broccoli, and slice the peppers before you make the pork. That way you'll be able to cook the "noodles" in a flash, while the pork is steamy hot.
- Substitute pineapple, orange, or pear juice for the apricot juice.
- Mirin is a sweet rice vinegar; it has a unique flavor, but it can be left out in a pinch.

50/50

Substitute tempeh, extra-firm tofu, or extra broccoli for a portion of the pork. Cook up your pork and nonmeat substitute separately and divide the apricot glaze over them.

Sweet + Sour Cabbage Noodles with Octopus

MAKES 4 SERVINGS

———

500↓

I get it; you're probably not cooking up octopus every night. And hey, if you want to serve up some chicken, fish, or pork with these Sweet + Sour Cabbage Noodles then by all means be my guest, they will go great with the Asian inspired "noodles!" But, if you have a little extra time and want to try something new, you will find that making octopus is as easy as boiling potatoes. This book is all about giving you a range of meal options, easy things for those busy nights along with dishes that push you a little, getting you to conquer a new ingredient or technique. So try this, or don't, heck it's your kitchen after all.

4 octopus tentacles (about 1½ pounds)

4 cups chicken stock

3 tablespoons olive oil

½ teaspoon smoked paprika

1¾ teaspoons kosher salt

1 medium head green cabbage (about 2½ pounds)

3 garlic cloves, minced

1 tablespoon peeled and grated fresh ginger

¼ cup rice wine vinegar

3 tablespoons brown sugar

2 tablespoons soy sauce

1½ teaspoons sriracha sauce

Finely grated zest and juice of 1 lime

4 tablespoons water

1 tablespoon cornstarch

½ cup sour cream

½ cup thinly sliced scallions, green parts only

1. Put the octopus and stock in a medium saucepan, adding water, if necessary, to keep the octopus submerged. Bring to a simmer over medium heat and cook until the octopus is easily pierced with a sharp knife, 60 to 90 minutes. Flip the octopus over from time to time as it will tend to float. (Testing for doneness is just like testing a potato.)

2. Meanwhile, cut the cabbage into ½- to ¾-inch-thick slices and separate them into ribbons. Heat 2 tablespoons of the oil in a large deep skillet over medium-high heat. Stir in the cabbage and 1½ teaspoons of

the salt and cook until the cabbage is slightly wilted but not mushy, about 5 minutes, stirring occasionally. Stir in the garlic and ginger and cook until fragrant, 3 to 4 minutes more. Stir in the vinegar, sugar, soy sauce, and 1 teaspoon of the sriracha and cook for 2 minutes.

3. When the octopus is done, lift it from the pot. If the tentacles are joined, cut them apart. Whisk together the remaining 1 tablespoon oil, the paprika, and the remaining ¼ teaspoon of the salt in a large bowl. Add the octopus and stir to coat.

4. In a small bowl, combine the cornstarch and 2 tablespoons of the water and whisk until dissolved. Add the lime zest and lime juice and then stir the slurry into the cabbage, mixing well. Cook until the sauce thickens, 2 to 3 minutes. Reduce the heat to low and keep the mixture warm while you finish the octopus.

5. To make a sour cream drizzle, mix the sour cream with the remaining ½ teaspoon sriracha and 2 tablespoons water in a small bowl. If you like, transfer the drizzle to a small squeeze bottle for serving.

6. Preheat a grill pan over high heat. Add the octopus and cook until it is slightly charred and crispy in spots, 2 to 3 minutes per side. The octopus is already cooked through, you are just giving it some texture and smokiness by grilling it. To serve, divide the cabbage noodles equally among four plates and place a tentacle atop each portion. Drizzle with the sour cream mixture and scatter the scallions on top.

Keep It Simple

- If you have to buy a whole octopus, remove the head before cooking.
- As you can see, octopus is actually pretty easy to cook, but if you're still a bit squeamish feel free to serve some grilled chicken or salmon on top of these noodles. Seared tofu is delicious also, and makes this a vegetarian recipe.
- I love the flavor of sriracha, but your favorite hot sauce will be just as tasty.

Nikki's Classic Tomato Sauce

MAKES 10 CUPS SAUCE

500↓ | FF

The first thing my husband and I ever cooked together was tomato sauce. We took his brother Clay's recipe and followed it to a T, Googling every step as we were convinced we were doing it wrong—and many times we really were doing it wrong. Since that day I have made tomato sauce more times than I can count, and I have perfected my recipe along the way. This tomato sauce is rich and tomatoey and, to be modest—it's perfect! I make huge batches of it and freeze it in 1-cup amounts or I spread it over pasta and freeze that in individual containers for homemade frozen meals.

6 tablespoons extra-virgin olive oil

2 cups finely chopped yellow onions

4 garlic cloves, sliced

Five 28-ounce cans whole plum tomatoes (preferably San Marzano)

2 to 4 teaspoons salt

½ teaspoon ground black pepper

⅓ cup chopped fresh basil leaves

¼ teaspoon crushed red pepper flakes

1. Heat the oil in a large stockpot or Dutch oven over medium heat. Stir in the onions and garlic and cook until soft and very fragrant, 7 to 10 minutes.

2. Add the tomatoes, 2 teaspoons of the salt, and the black pepper to the pot and puree the mixture with an immersion blender. Cook until the mixture begins to simmer, partially cover, then reduce the heat to medium-low; you want the tomatoes to be bubbling but not bubbling over! Allow the mixture to simmer until it thickens into a sauce and has reduced almost by half, about 2 hours. Stir occasionally to ensure that the sauce at the bottom doesn't burn.

3. Stir in the basil and red pepper flakes and cook the sauce for 30 minutes more; the sauce should be nice and thick! Taste it, and if you wish, you can add up to 2 teaspoons more of salt.

Keep It Simple

- In a rush I have upped the heat to medium-high, being sure to stir more frequently so the sauce doesn't burn. Doing this gives me finished sauce in just 1½ hours.
- Make this a low-calorie sauce by using just 2 tablespoons oil, instead of all 6 tablespoons called for. Each cup of sauce will clock in at a lean 125 calories!

Make It Meaty

Add cooked, sliced sausage or meatballs to the sauce along with the basil. As it simmers for the last 30 minutes the sauce will become infused with the flavor of the meat.

Suggested Servings!

You can use this sauce for my Spaghetti Squash Stuffed with Mozzarella + Tiny Chicken Meatballs (page 231) and my Three-Cheese Zucchini Involtini (page 247) or in any other recipe that is in need of a killer homemade tomato sauce.

Cabbage + Brussels Sprouts

Cabbage and Brussels sprouts are closely related and they come from the same happy family as broccoli and cauliflower. And like many of the veggies in that family, they are both great cancer-fighting foods. Cabbage has actually been shown to reduce breast cancer tumors— talk about an added benefit to eating a tasty cabbage dinner. But a lot of people have the occasional coleslaw or mushy steamed Brussels sprouts and that's the limit to their cabbage and Brussels sprouts experience. What they don't know is that these guys can do SO much more. Cabbage can be folded into nachos, included in killer grilled cheese sandwiches, smothered in Buffalo sauce and fried, or made into noodles. And of course, it still makes one hell of a coleslaw. And Brussels Sprouts? Roasted with bacon is nice, but I'm talking about wilting them on top of pizza, tossing them with creamy carbonara and pears, and smothering them in a pomegranate vinaigrette. That's how you show off this underappreciated vegetable family.

Recipe List

Mushrooms

Mushrooms come in all shapes and sizes, and while I like to use specific ones for their texture or subtle taste differences, most mushrooms are interchangeable. However, I admit I tend to turn away from the cheaper white button variety and use types like shiitakes, cremini, and portobellos for the extra depth of their flavor. But because the mushrooms in many of my dishes are smothered in sauces or heavily spiced, you really can substitute button mushrooms in these recipes and no one will be the wiser. And when you do, you'll actually be eating the best mushroom for your immune system: While all mushrooms are great anti-inflammatories, button mushrooms are actually at the top of that list. So go ahead and have mushrooms for dinner, and while you're at it, have them for breakfast and as an appetizer, too. They mimic the flavor and texture of meat and add an umami flavor, which is totally unique, making them a truly "Fun-gi" (Fun Guy, get it?! Yeah, it's lame, oh well).

Recipe List

Spaghetti Squash "Mac" + Cheese
with Green Chiles + Creole Chicken

MAKES 4 SERVINGS

—

FF

I knew I needed to bring my *Meat on the Side* point of view to my show, *Junk Food Flip.* When our job was to flip mac and cheese into something healthy, I knew I had a secret weapon. I wanted to bring veggies to the party, to make the dish spectacular. So I made my first spaghetti squash "mac" and cheese. We served it to hundreds of people who had no idea they were eating a vegetable, but they did know that it was creamy, rich, and crazy good. Now it is a staple in my house, and this version with green chiles, creole chicken, and tomatoes takes it to the next level. It's my go-to dinner when I want to "indulge."

2 tablespoons olive oil

2½ teaspoons kosher salt, plus more as needed

2 to 3 boneless skinless chicken breast halves (about 1 pound total)

1½ teaspoons Creole or Cajun seasoning blend

1 medium spaghetti squash (about 3 pounds)

2 tablespoons unsalted butter

3 garlic cloves, minced

3 scallions, thinly sliced (keep the white and green parts separate)

Two 4-ounce cans green chiles

2 tablespoons all-purpose flour

1½ cups whole milk

1 cup shredded sharp cheddar cheese (4 ounces)

1 cup shredded Pepper Jack cheese (4 ounces)

2 medium tomatoes, coarsely chopped

1. Preheat the oven to 400°F. Add 1 tablespoon of the oil, ½ teaspoon of the salt, and the Creole seasoning to a resealable food storage bag large enough to hold the chicken; mush together. Add the chicken and turn the bag over several times to coat the chicken with the seasoning. Refrigerate.

2. Cut the squash in half lengthwise. Using a soupspoon, scoop out the seeds and discard them. Arrange the squash, cut side up, on a rimmed baking sheet. Drizzle the remaining 1 tablespoon oil evenly over each

piece and then sprinkle them with 1 teaspoon of the salt. Bake the squash until the flesh is tender and can be easily separated with the tines of a fork, 35 to 40 minutes.

3. While the squash bakes, make the cheese sauce: Melt the butter in a large deep skillet over medium heat. Stir in the garlic, scallion whites, and ½ teaspoon of the salt and cook until fragrant and tender, about 5 minutes. (You don't want the butter or garlic to burn, so reduce the heat if either starts to brown). Stir in the chiles and cook 2 minutes more.

4. Add the flour to the skillet and cook for 2 minutes, whisking constantly. Pour in the milk and whisk or stir furiously to blend everything. Cook until the sauce has thickened, 3 to 5 minutes. Meanwhile, using a dinner fork, gently separate the squash flesh into spaghetti-like strands; you can leave the strands in the squash shells until you need them.

5. Add the cheddar and Jack cheeses to the sauce and stir until melted. Add the squash strands and ½ teaspoon of the remaining salt and stir well. Taste the mixture and add up to 1 more teaspoon salt if you wish. Reduce the heat to low so the mixture stays warm while you cook the chicken.

6. Preheat a grill pan over medium heat. Add the chicken and cook until lightly browned on both sides and no longer pink in the center, about 10 minutes, turning once. Transfer the chicken to a cutting board and let rest for 2 to 3 minutes; cut it into bite-size pieces. Sprinkle the cut tomatoes with a touch of salt.

7. To serve, divide the squash mixture equally among four plates. Top each with some chicken, tomatoes, and scallion greens, dividing them equally.

Keep It Simple

- You can use a combination of any cheese you like, along with cheddar and Pepper Jack. Mozzarella, fontina, Parmesan, and Gruyère are all great for cheese sauce.
- The green chiles are readily available in every grocery store; just look next to the taco sauce or beans. They are just roasted diced green peppers, but they add big flavor.
- You can make this recipe even leaner by using 1 percent milk and a low-fat cheddar. The moisture and sweetness of the squash easily make up for the lower fat content.
- If you don't have a seasoning blend try a combination of equal parts garlic powder, onion powder, paprika, and dried thyme or dried oregano.

FF

Yes, you are about to put a big plate of squash in front of your kids (and yourself), but I promise no one will know because all you taste is delicious cheesy goodness. Leave out the green chiles and use all cheddar for a milder taste. Try this; it's going to be a HIT!

Light Meals

Soups

Celery + Pear Soup

MAKES 4 SERVINGS

500↓ | FF

One of my favorite people, my sister Christina is also one buff chick. She could easily beat me up, so I make sure to keep on her good side by always making her my favorite dishes. To stay in such good shape she is obviously a smart eater; she always seems to be dipping celery into hummus. Celery is a healthy snack, but what she doesn't know is that it can take on so much more than hummus. It can be the basis of a refined soup with a fresh, light flavor that is perfectly balanced with pears and goat cheese and finished with roasted chopped celery for texture. The only reason my sister would beat me up now is to claim the leftovers, but I know better—they're all hers.

3 tablespoons unsalted butter

4 cups coarsely chopped celery

1 medium Vidalia onion, coarsely chopped

1 bay leaf

2 pears, peeled, cored and coarsely chopped

1 tablespoon fresh thyme leaves

2½ teaspoons kosher salt

4 cups chicken stock or vegetable stock

2 ounces soft goat cheese, plus more for garnish

¼ cup chopped hazelnuts

½ pear, cored and thinly sliced lengthwise, for garnish

1. Preheat the oven (or a toaster oven) to 450°F.

2. Melt the butter in a medium saucepan over medium heat. Add 3½ cups of the celery, the onion, and bay leaf and cook until the vegetables are slightly softened, 5 to 7 minutes.

3. Add the chopped pears, thyme, and salt to the vegetables and stir to mix. Pour in the stock, bring to a simmer, and cook until the vegetables and pears are tender, about 10 minutes, remove the bay leaf and add the cheese. Using an immersion blender, puree the soup and then cook for 20 to 25 minutes more to reduce it slightly and intensify the flavor.

Sweet Potato +
Butternut Squash Soup
(p. 184)

Celery + Pear Soup

4. Meanwhile, spread the remaining ½ cup celery on a rimmed baking sheet and roast in the oven until charred and tender, 20 minutes.

5. Ladle the soup into individual bowls and divide the roasted celery and hazelnuts equally over the tops. Crumble some additional goat cheese and scatter over the tops along with a few pear slices and serve.

Keep It Simple

• Swap the hazelnuts with almonds, cashews, or pine nuts, or omit, as you prefer.

• To make this soup completely vegetarian, simply use the vegetable stock listed as an alternative to the chicken stock.

• Keep the toppings simple and use just goat cheese; it adds the most flavor.

FF

The flavor of this soup is mild and slightly sweet—great for the whole family. To make it more familiar to your kids, change the toppings to croutons and a sprinkle of shredded mozzarella.

Cauliflower Soup with Pancetta + Pine Nut Hash

MAKES 6 SERVINGS

500↓ | 50/50

For *Food Network Star* I made dishes that take hours in minutes, completely put myself out there, tears and all, and allowed myself to be judged by the people I respected the most—and I did it all on national TV. I went without support from my family and friends, lived in a hotel, and spent nights stressing over the smallest critique. Yet my experiences from it make up some of my fondest memories. And it all started with Episode 1, where, with shaking hands, I made a Cauliflower Soup with Pancetta + Pine Nut Hash. Bobby Flay LOVED it and I have a feeling you will, too.

Cauliflower Soup

8 tablespoons (1 stick) unsalted butter, cut into pieces

1 large parsnip, coarsely chopped

1 yellow onion, coarsely chopped

1 potato, coarsely chopped

4 garlic cloves, sliced

1 medium head cauliflower (about 2 pounds), stem removed, coarsely chopped

2 quarts chicken stock

2 teaspoons kosher salt

¼ teaspoon ground nutmeg

1 tablespoon finely chopped fresh thyme leaves

Finely grated zest of 1 lemon

Pancetta + Pine Nut Hash

⅓ cup chopped pancetta or bacon

1 tablespoon olive oil (if needed)

1 potato, finely chopped

¼ cup pine nuts

2 tablespoons chopped fresh flat-leaf parsley

¼ teaspoon sweet paprika

½ teaspoon kosher salt, or more as needed

Cauliflower Soup

1. Melt the butter in a stockpot or large saucepan over medium heat and cook until browned, about 5 minutes. (You want to brown the butter to give the soup a really deep, nutty flavor.)

2. Add the parsnips, onion, potato, and garlic to the pot and cook until the veggies are tender and lightly browned, 7 to 10 minutes more.

3. Add the cauliflower, stock, and salt to the pot and stir to combine. Reduce the heat to medium-low, cover the pot, and cook until the cauliflower is very tender and mashable, about 20 minutes. Meanwhile, make the Pancetta + Parsnip Hash.

4. To finish, using an immersion blender, puree the soup in the stockpot (or transfer it in batches to a blender or food processor). Stir in the nutmeg, thyme, and lemon zest. Ladle the soup into six bowls and top each serving with a spoonful of the hash.

Pancetta + Pine Nut Hash

Preheat a medium skillet over medium heat. Add the pancetta and cook until crisp and all the fat has been rendered, about 5 minutes. If there is not enough fat to cook the potato, add the oil. Add the potato and cook until browned and tender, 6 to 8 minutes. Stir in the pine nuts, parsley, and paprika and cook until the pine nuts are golden brown, about 3 minutes. Taste the hash and add the salt as needed.

Keep It Simple

A parsnip is like a spicy carrot, it not only adds nice flavor but also keeps the soup white. But feel free to replace it with a more readily available carrot if you like. Add stock or water at any point to thin out a too-thick soup, including when reheating leftovers. But if a soup is too thin, just continue to cook it; as it simmers the water will evaporate and it will thicken.

50/50

Use vegetable stock instead of chicken stock and top only your non-vegetarian portions with the hash. A sprinkle of smoked paprika is nice on the vegetarian servings or make the hash without pancetta.

Sweet Potato + Butternut Squash Soup

MAKES 6 SERVINGS

500↓ | Make It Meaty

My husband is my official taste-tester. The price to him for eating a tasty *Meat on the Side* meal is that he must give a full report on every aspect of the dish. I bombard him with questions until he almost regrets this deal. One of his comments about this soup was "I don't know what I'm eating, but it's great." This soup is totally unique and you would never find anything like it in a can. With a couple of fun spices and the addition of peanut butter and vinegar, you end up with an Indian-inspired soup that is Evan-approved. He may not have known exactly what he was eating, but let me tell you, he ate every last bite.

2 medium sweet potatoes

1 small butternut squash

2 tablespoons olive oil

2 leeks, white and pale green parts only, coarsely chopped

4 garlic cloves, sliced

5 to 6 cups chicken stock or vegetable stock

3 tablespoons peanut butter

1 teaspoon ground turmeric

1 teaspoon ground cumin

½ teaspoon ground coriander

2 tablespoons sriracha sauce

2 tablespoons red wine vinegar

2 tablespoons chopped fresh cilantro

1. Peel the sweet potatoes and cut them into 1-inch cubes. Peel the squash. Cut it in half lengthwise and then, using a soupspoon, scoop out the seeds. Chop the flesh into 1-inch cubes. Clean any fibers from the seeds and spread the seeds out on a rimmed baking sheet; set aside.

2. Heat the oil in a large saucepan over medium heat. Stir in the leeks and garlic and cook until tender and fragrant, about 7 minutes.

3. Preheat the oven to 400°F.

4. Add the squash, sweet potatoes, and 4 cups of the stock to the pan with the leeks and bring to a boil. Reduce the heat so the stock is simmering and cook until the squash and potatoes are very tender and easily squished with a spoon, 25 to 35 minutes.

5. When the oven is preheated, bake the squash seeds until they are brown, 7 to 10 minutes. Set aside.

6. Using an immersion blender, puree the soup (or transfer it in batches to a blender or food processor). Then reduce the heat to low and gradually stir in 1 to 2 cups of the remaining stock, adding only enough to give the soup your preferred consistency. Add the peanut butter, turmeric, cumin, coriander, sriracha, and vinegar and stir until the peanut butter has dissolved and the soup is heated through, 2 to 3 minutes.

7. To serve, ladle the soup into six individual bowls. Top each with 1 teaspoon of the cilantro and a sprinkling of the toasted seeds.

Keep It Simple

If you don't have and don't want to invest in a bunch of spices that you don't think you'll use very often, replace the turmeric, cumin, and coriander with 1½ teaspoons curry powder.

Make It Meaty

You can add Tiny Chicken Meatballs (page 223) to this recipe. Halved Eggplant "Meatballs" (page 196) are good, too.

Eggplant Fans
with Caesar Dressing + Bread Crumbs

MAKES 2 SERVINGS; DOUBLE THE RECIPE AS YOU WISH

10-in-20 | Make It Meaty

When I was young I was obsessed with paper fans. They were so elegant and exotic and I often pictured myself grown-up, in a long dress, fanning myself on some grand terrace. Obviously I had recently watched *Gone with the Wind* or something along that line. Well my vision never exactly came true, but I still do love fans, eggplant fans that is. ;) A couple of cuts with your knife, and you have the most elegant light meal or side dish. The eggplant becomes tender and slightly crispy and, with the creamy dressing and bread crumbs, it is indulgent and comforting. These eggplant fans are much better than any paper fan and obviously much tastier.

4 small eggplants, such as Chinese eggplant or
    fairytale eggplant
1 tablespoon olive oil
½ teaspoon kosher salt
¼ teaspoon ground black pepper
2 tablespoons unsalted butter

1½ cups coarsely ground homemade bread crumbs
    (see Appendix, page 259)
2 tablespoons chopped fresh flat-leaf parsley, plus
    more for garnish
½ cup Caesar dressing (see page 71)

1. Preheat the oven to 450°F. Line a baking sheet with parchment paper or spray it with cooking oil.

2. To prepare the fans, cut each eggplant lengthwise, from the base up to the stem, into several ¼-inch-thick leaves. Be sure not to cut all the way through the stem end—you want the top to remain attached. Arrange the eggplants on the baking sheet, fanning the leaves as shown in the photo. Brush the oil evenly over the fans and sprinkle them with the salt and pepper. When the oven is hot, bake the eggplants until they can easily be pierced with a fork, 15 to 20 minutes.

3. While the eggplants bake, melt the butter in a medium skillet over medium heat. Stir in the bread crumbs until they are evenly coated. Then stir in the parsley, tossing to combine, and let cook until the crumbs are golden brown and crunchy, about 5 minutes.

4. To serve, transfer an eggplant fan to each plate. Pour the dressing evenly over each and sprinkle with the bread crumbs. Scatter some chopped parsley on top.

Keep It Simple

• Can't find small eggplants? Large ones can work just fine. Cut large eggplants in half lengthwise through the stem creating two even halves of the eggplant (if your eggplant is super large you can cut these halves in half). Then cut into ¼-inch-thick leaves as instructed, fan the leaves, and cook, cut side down.

• You can always use a store-bought Caesar dressing to make this in a snap. Or, if you prefer, you can use blue cheese or ranch dressing.

Make It Meaty

Serve this with strips of cooked chicken breast, and drizzle the dressing and bread crumbs over the chicken as well as the eggplant.

Cabbage + Pear Galette

———

500↓

My mother is a lovely person, but not the best cook in the world. Being a gourmet home chef was not exactly a priority when there were four kids fighting at the table and one (me) trying to James Bond her way away from it. Now I try to encourage my mother to try new things, but I know what she would say about this recipe: "A what? A gaaaleettee? I can't make that." But here's the thing, she can. It is just a tart or pie thing that you make free-form, no pan required. It's like making a pizza and folding up the edges. Everyone, including Lori Dinki, can make beautiful meals like this Cabbage + Pear Galette.

2 tablespoons unsalted butter

1 medium yellow onion, very thinly sliced

2 cups packed very thinly sliced cabbage (a mix of red and green)

1 teaspoon kosher salt

2 teaspoons chopped fresh flat-leaf parsley, plus more for garnish

½ teaspoon chopped fresh tarragon leaves, plus more for garnish

1 pear (not peeled)

One 11-inch pie crust (not baked)

2 tablespoons peach jam

¾ cup crumbled soft goat cheese (3 ounces)

1 large egg

1 tablespoon water

1. Preheat the oven to 400°F.

2. Melt the butter in a large skillet over medium heat. Stir in the onion and cook for 3 minutes. Stir in the cabbage and salt and continue to cook until the veggies are soft but not mushy, 3 to 5 minutes. Add the parsley and tarragon and stir to combine. Remove the skillet from the heat.

3. Cut the pear lengthwise in half and core it; then slice each piece crosswise into thin half-moons. Lay the pie crust on a baking sheet. Arrange half the pear in a circle in the center of the dough, leaving a 1½-inch border around the edge.

4. Put the jam in a small microwave-safe bowl and microwave on high for 15 seconds. Brush half the jam over the pear slices on the pie crust. Scatter half the cheese over the slices and then spoon the cabbage mixture over the top. Arrange the rest of the pear slices over the cabbage, brush with the remaining jam, and scatter the rest of the cheese over the top.

5. Fold the border up over the filling, pleating the crust at intervals onto itself as needed. Whisk together the egg and water in a small bowl and brush over the exposed crust. Bake the galette in the preheated oven until the crust is golden brown and the cheese has browned in spots, about 30 minutes. Sprinkle with the extra parsley and tarragon, and cut into wedges and serve!

Keep It Simple

- The egg wash (egg and water mixture) makes the crust super pretty, but it's only for presentation purposes so feel free to skip it.
- You can use any jam you have on hand: pear, raspberry, and apple all work fine.
- I like a touch of tarragon's licorice flavor in this galette. But you can do all parsley for a milder flavor, or a combination of parsley and basil or thyme.
- My grocery store sells shredded cabbage in the produce section for almost the same price as whole, so it's easy to pick up a little red and a little green, but feel free to use all red or all green in this recipe.

MAD FOR MANDOLINES

My husband and I love watching cooking competition shows, but we always cringe when someone pulls out a mandoline. This slide-and-slice device that let's you push ingredients under a fixed blade to yield pieces of even thickness is a dangerous piece of equipment, and it's made even more dangerous when wielded by shaking hands and people under time constraints. But used safely it is really irreplaceable and invaluable. When slicing something superthin as only a mandoline can do, you transform your food. Suddenly very thinly sliced radishes and red onions add the perfect amount of bitterness and acid and don't overtake a dish. Zucchini and other veggies are slid through the julienne attachment and come out as perfect strands of "spaghetti" on the other side. And there is no other way to get properly sized potato, parsnip, or beet chips. A mandoline can turn you from home cook to executive chef in an instant, and you can get the same one that all the fancy chefs use for around $20. So make someone get you a mandoline this Christmas, or just call this Tuesday a holiday and gift one to yourself!

Leek + Apple Tarte Tatin

MAKES 2 SERVINGS; DOUBLE THE RECIPE AS YOU WISH

10-in-30 | 500↓ | Make It Meaty

I've always challenged myself to make my dreams come true. I dreamt of an amazing husband and got exactly that (I know, I'm totally corny), I dreamt of sharing my food with millions of people, and this Leek + Apple Tarte Tatin is what my food dreams are made of. A tarte Tatin is a pie baked upside down, named after the Tatin sisters whose apple version became famous. In mine puff pastry is laid over leeks and apples. Flip it after baking: the result is a caramelized filling that has baked right into a soft yet chewy crust. Drizzled with honey and scattered with goat cheese, this tarte Tatin proves that dreams do come true.

5 to 6 small leeks (about 2¼ pounds)

3 tablespoons unsalted butter

½ teaspoon kosher salt

½ Granny Smith apple, cored and cut into ⅛-inch-thick half-moons

1 teaspoon finely chopped fresh thyme leaves, plus more for garnish

2 tablespoons honey

1 sheet frozen puff pastry, thawed

1 ounce soft goat cheese, crumbled into largish pieces

1. Preheat the oven to 400°F.

2. Cut off and discard the root and darker green leafy end of the leeks. Then cut each leek crosswise into ¾-inch pieces. Add these to a bowl of cold water and gently separate the layers to remove any grit, but keep the segments intact. Rinse in a colander and then pat dry with a kitchen towel.

3. Melt the butter in a 9-inch omelet pan over medium-high heat. Arrange the leek segments upright (with a cut end down) in the pan. Sprinkle the salt over the leeks and let them cook, undisturbed, until they begin to brown on the bottom, about 5 minutes. Turn all the leek segments over and immediately remove the pan from the heat. Sprinkle the thyme over the leeks and arrange the apples in a single layer on top. Drizzle 1 tablespoon of the honey over the apples.

4. Cut the puff pastry into a 10-inch diameter circle. (Most puff pastry comes in 10-inch squares so really, all you need to do is cut off the corners; this circle doesn't need to be all that precise.) Lay the pastry over the omelet pan and tuck the edges down between the pan and the leeks to enclose the apples and leeks. The edge of the pastry should be touching the bottom of the pan. It's okay if the pastry folds over on itself a bit. Use a paring knife to cut several slits in the top of the pastry so the tart can vent as it bakes.

5. Bake the tart until the pastry is golden brown, 18 to 20 minutes. Then transfer the pan to a wire rack to cool for 5 minutes.

6. Invert a plate over the tart in the pan. Using oven mitts, and holding the plate and pan together, quickly flip them over, so that the tart drops onto the plate. Lift off the pan. If any leek segments have stuck to the pan, place them back in the tart. Drizzle the remaining 1 tablespoon honey over the tart, sprinkle with a little more thyme, scatter the cheese over all. Cut the tart into wedges and serve warm.

Keep It Simple

- I like Granny Smith apples because they hold up well when cooked, but several other apples would also be fine in this recipe. You can experiment to see whether you like it better with tart or sweet apples.
- Substitute feta, queso fresco, or little dollops of cream cheese for the goat cheese—whichever appeals most to you.
- If you get off on your timing while prepping, put the thawed pastry in the refrigerator until you are ready to use it. It should always be as cold as possible.

Make It Meaty

Cook up 3 ounces of finely diced pancetta in the pan before you begin step 3. Then remove them, add the leeks, and continue the step, but before you add the apple slices, sprinkle the pancetta over the leeks. Continue with the rest of the recipe, and enjoy the porky, salty bite of your Leek + Apple Tarte Tatin.

Eggplant "Meatballs"

MAKES ABOUT FORTY 1-INCH BALLS

500↓ | FF

I make huge batches of these "meatballs" and use them with everything. Top any pasta with them, like Brussels Sprouts + Pear Carbonara (page 147) or Spaghetti Squash "Mac" and Cheese with Green Chilies (page 176); throw them on a hero roll with a bit of tomato or eggplant sauce and some grated Parmesan; toss them with Three-Onion Rice (page 216); or use them to make a salad heartier, like Escarole Salad with Pesto Dressing on page 74.

1 medium eggplant (about 1 pound)	4 garlic cloves
3 tablespoons olive oil	1 teaspoon fresh thyme leaves
10 ounces cremini mushrooms, coarsely chopped	½ teaspoon fresh rosemary leaves
1 small yellow onion, coarsely chopped	1½ cups panko bread crumbs
1 poblano chile, seeds and ribs removed, coarsely chopped	1 large egg
	1½ teaspoons kosher salt

1. Preheat the oven to 450°F. Grease a clean baking sheet or line it with parchment paper. Cut the eggplant in half lengthwise and place, cut side up, on a rimmed baking sheet. Drizzle 1 tablespoon of the oil over the cut surfaces. When the oven is hot, bake the eggplants until tender to the touch, 25 to 30 minutes. Set the eggplants aside to cool, but leave the oven on.

2. Add the mushrooms, onion, poblano, garlic, thyme, and rosemary to a large food processor and pulse until finely chopped. Stir as necessary and do not overprocess; you want small pieces but not mush.

3. Heat the remaining 2 tablespoons oil in a large skillet over medium-high heat. Stir in the chopped vegetables and sauté until tender and any moisture they give off has evaporated, 7 to 10 minutes.

4. Meanwhile, using a soupspoon, scoop the flesh of the cooled eggplants into the food processor. Process until pureed; you should have about ¾ cup eggplant puree. When the vegetables in the skillet are cooked, stir the eggplant puree into them and mix well. Transfer the mixture to a large bowl.

5. When the mixture in the bowl is cool enough to handle, add the bread crumbs, egg, and salt to it and mix well until everything comes together. Pinch a walnut-size amount between your fingers and then roll it into a 1-inch ball; repeat until all the mixture is shaped into balls. Arrange the balls on the prepared baking sheet and bake in the still-heated oven until crisp and medium brown on the outside, 25 to 30 minutes.

6. Bake refrigerated balls at 400°F for 5 minutes and frozen balls for 10 minutes. Microwaving works, too, but gives you a softer texture.

FF

Serve these to your kids and after they gobble them up you will be in my debt forever—because your kids just ate a ball of veggies, and they liked it! They will especially like them if you pair the "meatballs" with their favorite pasta and sauce. These "meatballs" are even great with mac and cheese! (I just made myself really hungry, gotta go . . .)

Tomato + Pineapple Packets
with Sea Bass + Halloumi

MAKES 4 SERVINGS

500↓ | 50/50

Christmas is my favorite holiday; just imagine a house full of Dinkis hopped up on sugar and loud as hell with excitement. For us it's not so much about the actual gifts as it is about the surprise of it all, and we Dinkis love nothing more than a good surprise. So why not make our food a surprise? Mix up sweet yet contrasting flavors like tomatoes, pineapples, and poblanos, top with beautiful pieces of fish, and wrap up individual servings into the perfect little presents. Bake until saucy; then place a packet on each plate, ready to be opened and devoured. The colors, the bright flavors, and the aroma will officially make this the best present ever! To begin the gift-giving season, this recipe is my gift to you; I always give the best gifts.

8 ounces halloumi cheese

4 cups cherry tomatoes, 2 cups halved and the rest whole

2 cups fresh pineapple chunks (bite-size pieces)

2 poblano chiles, seeds and ribs removed, cut into bite-size pieces

¼ cup chopped fresh cilantro, plus more for garnish

Juice of 1 lemon

Finely grated zest and juice of 1 lime

2 teaspoons ground sumac

2 teaspoons kosher salt

4 Chilean sea bass fillets (about 4 ounces each)

4 teaspoons olive oil

1 lemon, cut into ¼-inch-thick rounds

Baguette slices, for dipping

1. Preheat the oven to 400°F.

2. Cut the cheese in half crosswise and pat it dry with paper towels. Heat a small nonstick skillet over medium-high heat. Add the cheese and sauté until golden on both sides, about 3 minutes per side. Transfer the cheese to a cutting board and cut it into bite-size pieces.

3. Combine the tomatoes, cooked cheese, pineapples, poblanos, chopped cilantro, lemon juice, lime zest, lime juice, sumac, and 1½ teaspoons of the salt in a large bowl and mix well.

4. Place 4 pieces of parchment paper or aluminum foil, each about 18 inches long, on a work surface. Spoon one-quarter of the tomato mixture onto the middle of each piece. Sprinkle the remaining ½ teaspoon salt evenly over the fish and then place 1 fillet atop each mound of the tomato mixture. Drizzle 1 teaspoon oil over each fillet. Divide the lemon slices over the fillets. Make each sheet of parchment into a sealed packet by folding up and crimping together the long edges and then folding each end up and over on itself, enclosing the filling.

5. Arrange the packets on a baking sheet. Place in the preheated oven and bake until the fish is just cooked through, 20 to 25 minutes. If you check the doneness of the fish and it's not ready, take the opportunity to baste the fish in the sauce that will have accumulated in the bottom of the packet.

6. To serve, place each packet on a dinner plate. Open each partway, sprinkle the contents with additional chopped cilantro, and pass bread for dipping at the table.

Keep It Simple

- Sumac adds a bright citrusy note; you can leave it out or use 1 teaspoon paprika instead.
- Halloumi is a unique cheese that holds its shape when heated; it is salty with a mild milky flavor. If you can't find it, add queso fresco or feta along with the cilantro after the packets are baked.
- Though not as pretty, using foil instead of parchment makes sealing up the packets a breeze and works just as well.

50/50

To make a vegetarian packet, simply omit the fish for a light meal, or omit the fish and add an extra 2 ounces of cheese or some browned tofu cubes.

Sticky Eggplant Rice Bowls

MAKES 4 SERVINGS

Make It Meaty

My friend Talia and I like to go out for marathon dinners, lots of courses and, of course, lots of sparkling wine. One of our favorite spots is a neighborhood sushi place that has just as many amazing cooked dishes as they do sushi, including my favorite, a warm, miso-glazed eggplant—it's sticky, sweet, and packed with flavor. I wanted to take on the challenge of mimicking that dish at home while only using a few ingredients from my fridge instead of the no doubt 20 plus they use at the restaurant. To accomplish this I focused on full-flavored components like apricot jam, fish sauce, and sherry vinegar to create a rich glaze that pairs beautifully with the eggplant. Now all you need is a glass of Prosecco and a friend like Talia and you've got one incredible night.

1 stalk lemongrass

2 cups apricot jam

½ cup beef stock, plus more as needed

⅓ cup sherry vinegar

1 tablespoon fish sauce

1 tablespoon soy sauce

2½ cups water

1¼ cups long-grain white rice

1 tablespoon unsalted butter

1½ teaspoons kosher salt

1 tablespoon olive oil

1 large eggplant (about 1 pound),
     cut into bite-size pieces

1 tablespoon white vinegar

4 large eggs

¼ cup finely chopped fresh chives

1. Trim the ends of the lemongrass stalk and remove a couple of the outer layers. Then slice it crosswise into thin rounds. Add to a small saucepan along with the jam, ½ cup stock, sherry vinegar, fish sauce, and soy sauce. Place over medium heat and cook to a glaze consistency, about 20 minutes. (You want the sauce to be pourable, if it gets very thick, stir in more stock.) Strain the sauce into a clean saucepan and place over low heat.

2. While the sauce is cooking, prepare the rice: Put the water and rice in a second small saucepan and bring to a boil over medium heat. Reduce the heat to medium-low, cover the pan, and let simmer until the

rice is cooked through but still firm, 10 to 20 minutes, or as indicated in the package directions. When done, remove from the heat and stir in the butter and 1 teaspoon of the salt.

3. Heat the oil in a large skillet over medium heat. Add the eggplant and sprinkle with the remaining ½ teaspoon salt and stir to combine. Sauté until the eggplant is tender and slightly brown, about 5 minutes.

4. Add 2 inches of water to a large saucepan or deep skillet and bring to a boil. Reduce the heat and adjust to maintain a slow simmer. Add the white vinegar. Crack an egg into a small bowl or a coffee cup and then slide it into the water; repeat right away with each remaining egg. Cook the eggs until the whites are firm, but the yolks are still soft, 4 to 6 minutes. Using a slotted spoon, transfer the eggs to paper towels to drain.

5. To serve, stir the sauce into the skillet with the eggplant and toss to combine. Divide the rice equally among four bowls and spoon the eggplant mixture equally on top. Place a poached egg on each serving and scatter 1 tablespoon of the chives over the top.

Keep It Simple

• Many types of jams and vinegars will work for the sauce; you can try orange or peach for the jam and red wine, white wine, or apple cider for the vinegar. Also any stock will work, so you can use vegetable stock to make this dish vegetarian.
• Fish sauce is usually less than $2 a bottle and really adds a unique flavor that can't be replicated. But if you're in a pinch, leave it out.

Make It Meaty

Cook up half a spicy or mild sausage per person and toss with the eggplant (if you're serving some vegetarians at the same meal, assemble their bowls first). Or grill up 4 large shrimp per person, chop, and scatter atop the bowl.

Winter Squash

Winter squash have the density of root vegetables and the sweetness of carrots, you can turn them into fantastic purees to add to dishes (think fall soups to cozy up to on a chilly night), you can roast pieces of them for supersweet and smoky additions to salads and pastas, or you can stuff them with flavors we all love, like tomato sauce and cheese. Most winter squash are interchangeable in recipes. Butternut, acorn, kabocha, and pumpkin are all similar in their mild taste and sweet firm flesh. The only exception to the rule is spaghetti squash. Although it tastes similar to the rest, its texture is very different: It gives you long spaghetti-like strands when cooked, making it great for a play on "Mac" and Cheese. All winter squash have seeds that can be toasted for a great crunchy finish to salads, soups, and lots of other dishes. And best of all, these eatable gourds are low in calories, high in fiber and vitamin A, and inexpensive. Plus they stay fresh for months, yes MONTHS, making them the perfect thing to have on hand.

Recipe List

Cauliflower

I LOVE cooking with cauliflower, I could write a whole book on it. Cauliflower is one of my favorite veggies. Now I know what you're thinking, you're looking at a head of bumpy cauliflower, no color, no pizzazz, and you're thinking, how can THIS be a favorite? Well, it's because it is so versatile. With its mild taste and amazing texture you can literally do anything with cauliflower: roast it, puree it, grind it; use it to give body and flavor to soup, or substitute it for conventional pizza dough (hey, no carbs). And forget your morning OJ; if I had my way you'd be eating cauliflower every AM. One serving of cauliflower has 77 percent of your daily requirement of vitamin C, along with a plethora of antioxidants and other cancer-fighting properties. It's also a great source of protein. It's time to look at cauliflower in a whole new light.

Recipe List

Roasted Grape, Arugula + Goat Cheese Baked Potatoes

MAKES 4 BAKED POTATOES

──────

500↓

To ensure that all of my recipes turn out perfectly for you and not like a #PinterestFail, a lovely woman, Carol, helps me double-, triple-, and quadruple-check everything so we can be sure my recipes are clear, precise, and easy to follow. During one of our million conversations, she mentioned that her favorite light meal is a baked potato with olive oil, Romano cheese, and watercress. Well once you make me hungry for something I must have it, so that night I whipped up my version: a soft and well-seasoned potato with peppery arugula and roasted grapes that are insanely good, especially when mixed with honey and goat cheese.

4 Idaho potatoes, scrubbed and dried

2 tablespoons olive oil

1½ teaspoons kosher salt

2 cups red seedless grapes

¼ teaspoon ground black pepper

2 cups lightly packed, coarsely chopped arugula

4 ounces soft garlic and herb goat cheese log,

¼ cup honey

1. Preheat the oven to 400°F. Prick each potato with a fork 5 to 10 times. Rub 1 tablespoon of the oil over the potatoes and sprinkle them with ¼ teaspoon of the salt. Place them in the preheated oven, directly on the rack, and bake until they are soft when squeezed, 45 to 60 minutes.

2. Meanwhile, toss the grapes with the remaining 1 tablespoon oil, ¼ teaspoon of the salt, and the pepper on a rimmed baking sheet or in a medium baking dish. When the potatoes have about 20 minutes of baking time left, place the grapes in the oven. When the potatoes are done the grapes should be slightly shriveled and starting to burst open.

3. Slice each potato lengthwise, cutting about three-quarters of the way down. Push the ends of each toward the middle to open up a crevice. Divide it equally, sprinkle ½ teaspoon of the salt over the 4 crevices and then fluff each potato with a fork. Add one-quarter of the arugula to each potato and divide the

remaining ½ teaspoon salt over all 4 potatoes; fluff again to mix the potato flesh and the arugula (you want to try and salt the entire inside of the potato).

4. To serve, place each potato on a plate. Divide the cheese and grapes among them, filling the crevices, and then drizzle 1 tablespoon honey over each. Eat right away!

Main Meals

Lemongrass Fried Rice
with Yellow Pepper, Cucumber + Shrimp

MAKES 4 SERVINGS

50/50

Many of us go on autopilot at the grocery store and end up getting the same things every week. We don't often grab something new like say lemongrass. In fact you've probably seen this straw-like herb in a corner of the produce section or in a jar and thought, "I wonder who uses this?" Well, now you do! A common seasoning in Asian sautés and broths, lemongrass adds a totally unique flavor that will suddenly elevate any dish to an exotic level. I know it's not in your normal routine, but try it once (check out page 259 to learn some basic prep) and lemongrass just may be at the top of next week's shopping list.

2 stalks lemongrass, about ¾-inch thick at the base

3½ cups chicken stock

1½ cups long-grain white rice

3 tablespoons vegetable oil, plus more if needed

1 small yellow onion, coarsely chopped

4 garlic cloves, sliced

1½ teaspoons kosher salt

1 yellow bell pepper, cored, seeded, and coarsely chopped

1 teaspoon peeled and grated fresh ginger

½ English cucumber, finely chopped

2 teaspoons soy sauce

1 teaspoon fish sauce

½ teaspoon sesame oil

¾ cup thinly sliced scallions, green parts only

1 tablespoon olive oil

1 pound large shrimp (35), peeled and deveined

¼ teaspoon ground black pepper

Lemon half or wedges, for serving

1. Trim the ends of the lemongrass stalks and remove a couple of the outer layers. Using a heavy skillet or meat mallet, smash the stalks until they start to break apart, then cut them into 3-inch pieces. Combine the stock and lemongrass in a medium saucepan over medium heat, bring to a simmer, and let simmer for 10 minutes. Add the rice and bring to a boil. Reduce the heat to medium-low, cover the pan, and let simmer until the liquid has been absorbed and the rice is cooked through but still firm, 10 to 20 minutes, or as indicated in the package directions.

2. When the rice is done, spread it out on a large plate and pick out and discard the pieces of lemongrass. Transfer the rice to the refrigerator to cool and dry out for at least 30 minutes, or as long as possible; stir it occasionally. While it dries, heat the vegetable oil in a large skillet over medium heat and stir in the onion, garlic, and 1 teaspoon of the salt. Cook until the onion is tender, 5 to 7 minutes.

3. Add the bell pepper and ginger to the skillet and cook, stirring, for 3 minutes. Then stir in the cucumber, soy sauce, fish sauce, and sesame oil and cook for 2 minutes more. Increase the heat to medium-high, stir in the rice, and cook for 3 minutes more to heat through. If the rice sticks, try adding more vegetable oil. (Sticking is a sign that your rice may have been too wet when you added it to the pan, but even if it sticks a bit it will taste just as good in the end.) Stir all but a few of the scallions into the rice mixture and cover the pan to keep the rice warm while you cook the shrimp.

4. Heat the olive oil in a medium skillet over medium-high heat. Toss the shrimp with the remaining ½ teaspoon salt and the black pepper in a medium bowl. Add to the skillet and sauté until pink and slightly charred, turning once, about 4 minutes total.

5. As soon as the shrimp are done, divide the rice equally among four dinner plates. Mound one-quarter of the shrimp on top of each serving, scatter with the remaining scallions, and serve with a squeeze of lemon juice.

Keep It Simple

• The lemongrass makes this dish, hence the title. But if you can't find it, don't worry; you will still have a killer fried rice at the end. You can squeeze on a little extra lemon to mimic a bit of the lemongrass flavor.
• If you omit the fish sauce and sesame oil you are not going to get as deep and rich a flavor as you will when including them; however many fried rice recipes call for just soy sauce, so skip them for a simpler supper.

50/50

If you decide to leave the shrimp off some servings of this dish, I suggest adding some sautéed zucchini and some edamame instead. You can also serve this with a fried egg on top!

BBQ Broccoli + Chicken
over Three-Onion Rice

MAKES 2 SERVINGS; ABOUT 1½ CUPS SAUCE; DOUBLE THE RECIPE AS YOU WISH.

FF | 50/50

During summer weekends my husband becomes master of the grill, cooking up dinner as he takes on the mosquitoes and spiders that I desperately try to avoid. (Me? I'm taking a well-deserved break inside, enjoying a good book and chilled wine.) One night, he was on a mission to make the most perfect ribs. After concocting his signature rub and smoking his ribs to tender perfection, he felt that it was just wrong to finish with a store-bought barbecue sauce. So (with much coercion!), I got my butt off the couch and whipped up a BBQ sauce that is so good it could never come from a bottle. And turns out, it's just as tasty on broccoli as it is on ribs, and thus this recipe was born.

BBQ Sauce

1 tablespoon olive oil

1 small yellow onion, finely chopped

2 garlic cloves, minced

1 cup ketchup

¼ cup apple cider vinegar

2 tablespoons Worcestershire sauce

1 tablespoon molasses

1 teaspoon Dijon mustard

½ teaspoon ancho chili powder

¼ teaspoon chipotle chili powder

¼ teaspoon smoked paprika

Broccoli + Chicken

5 cups broccoli florets

2 teaspoons kosher salt

3 tablespoons olive oil

2 skinless, boneless chicken breast halves (about 3 ounces each, cut into 1-inch cubes)

Three-Onion Rice (page 217)

½ cup chopped fresh flat-leaf parsley

BBQ Sauce

1. Briefly heat the oil in a small saucepan over medium heat. Add the onion and garlic, and cook until tender and fragrant, 5 to 7 minutes.

2. Add the ketchup, vinegar, Worcestershire sauce, molasses, mustard, chili powders, and paprika to the onion mixture and stir to combine. Reduce the heat to low and allow the sauce to simmer for 30 minutes; it will become darker in color. While the sauce is simmering, make the Broccoli + Chicken (below). When the sauce is done, cover it and keep warm over low heat.

Broccoli + Chicken

1. Preheat the oven to 450°F.

2. Toss the broccoli with 1 teaspoon of the salt and 2 tablespoons of the oil in a large bowl and spread it out on a rimmed baking sheet. When the oven is preheated, roast the broccoli until tender and slightly charred around the edges, 15 to 20 minutes. Turn off the oven, but leave the broccoli in it with the door cracked open to keep the broccoli warm.

3. While the broccoli is roasting, sprinkle the chicken with the remaining 1 teaspoon salt. Heat a medium skillet over medium-high heat with the remaining 1 tablespoon oil. Add the chicken to the skillet and cook until lightly browned and cooked through, 5 to 7 minutes.

4. Add the broccoli to the skillet. Stir in some of the BBQ sauce; how much depends on your taste, so I suggest starting with about half and then adding more as you wish. Toss so everything is coated and then, if the broccoli has cooled, continue to cook the mixture briefly until it is hot again. Serve over Three-Onion Rice, garnished with the chopped parsley.

Keep It Simple
• The Three-Onion Rice takes longer to prep than the BBQ Broccoli + Chicken, so be sure to start it first.
• Making the BBQ sauce is easy, but to make this dinner SUPER quick, use store-bought sauce.
• No oven? No problem. Just sauté the broccoli in a pan instead of baking it.

FF
BBQ sauce is always a hit, but store-bought versions can be loaded with unnecessary sugar and preservatives. Making your own not only tastes better but also is better for you and your family.

50/50
• For oe vegetarian serving, decrease the amount of chicken by 3 ounces (1 breast half) and increase the broccoli by 2 cups. Divide the BBQ sauce accordingly.
• Tofu and many types of beans can replace the chicken, or used in addition.
• For a little extra protein, or as a substitute for the chicken, add a couple of scrambled eggs to the rice—like fried rice in Chinese cuisine.

Three-Onion Rice

MAKES 4 SERVINGS; HALVE THE RECIPE IF YOU WISH

500↓

Onions need to be "cleaned up" a bit before they take center stage. To make them a star you can cook them low and slow until their hidden sugars come out and transform them from bitter to sticky sweet and meaty, or you can fry them. In a flash you'll have a completely addictive super-crunchy texture. To really appreciate onions you have to choose the right ones for the job. For instance, scallions and chives have a delicate, mild onion flavor—perfect for topping. This rice combines all these things, sweet onions, crunchy onions and fresh onions, making you so in love with onions that you'll want to pull one right out of the earth and take a bite; but please don't— dirt tastes bad, but this rice, well this rice tastes VERY good!

2 tablespoons unsalted butter	1½ cups long-grain white rice
2 large Vidalia onions, thinly sliced	3 tablespoons canola oil
1 to 2 teaspoons kosher salt, plus more if desired	2 shallots, thinly sliced
3 cups chicken stock or water	4 scallions, green parts only, thinly sliced

1. Melt the butter in a large skillet over medium-low heat. Stir in the onions and 1 teaspoon of the salt. Cook, stirring only occasionally (you want to allow the onions to brown a bit before stirring them again) until the onions are very soft and medium-brown in color, 50 to 60 minutes.

2. Meanwhile, after the onions have cooked for 20 to 30 minutes, add the stock and rice to a medium saucepan and bring to a boil over medium heat. Reduce the heat to medium-low, cover the pan, and allow the rice to simmer until cooked through but still firm, 10 to 20 minutes, or as indicated in the package directions.

3. While the rice cooks, heat the oil in a small skillet over medium-high heat. Stir in the shallots and cook until browned, crisp, and sweet, 3 to 5 minutes. Using a slotted spoon, transfer the shallots to a paper towel–lined plate to drain.

4. When the onions are caramelized and the rice is done, stir the rice, along with the scallions, into the skillet with the onions and heat through. If you used water instead of chicken stock, add the remaining 1 teaspoon salt (or more as desired). Top with the crispy shallots and serve.

Keep It Simple

Cooking the rice in chicken stock makes the rice especially flavorful, but water will work also.

Serving Suggestions

Three-Onion Rice is the perfect complement to my BBQ Broccoli + Chicken (page 213), but I suggest making extra and pairing it with Eggplant "Meatballs" (page 196), or serving it instead of orzo in Beets + Scallops with Red Onion Jam (page 225). Or try whipping up a quick kale salad with vinaigrette and serving it on top of the rice along with some nuts and feta.

Potatoes, Tuna + Wheat Berries
with Garden-Fresh Tomato Sauce

MAKES 4 SERVINGS

———

50/50

With wheat berries you are getting some serious nutritional bang for your calorie buck. For every 100 calories of wheat berries you get about 4 grams of protein and 4 grams of fiber. Wheat berries are the most whole of whole grains—the actual seed of the wheat plant. They are not stripped of their outer layer the way barley or farro are. They are nutty and chewy and hold up very well when it comes to freezing or sitting for a long time in a soup. They are also great topped with seared tuna, crispy potatoes, and my Garden-Fresh Tomato Sauce. This dish is full of contrasting textures: soft and fatty tuna, brown and crisp potatoes and, of course, your new favorite grain: chewy wheat berries.

1¼ cups wheat berries

4 cups chicken stock

2 large Yukon gold potatoes (about 4 inches long)

2 tablespoons olive oil

1½ teaspoons kosher salt

¾ teaspoon ground black pepper

2 tuna steaks (6 to 8 ounces each)

2 cups hot Garden-Fresh Tomato Sauce (page 222)

Chopped fresh basil leaves, for garnish

1. Combine the wheat berries and stock in a medium saucepan, adding water, if necessary, so the berries are covered by at least 2 inches of liquid. Cover the pan and cook over medium heat until the berries are tender but chewy, 25 to 50 minutes. (The time will depend on the character of the berries, so check often after 25 minutes, or consult the package directions).

2. Meanwhile, trim the potatoes into a brick shape and then cut them into ½-inch-thick rectangles, each about 1½ × 3 inches; you should have 12 slices. Put the slices into a medium bowl, add 1 tablespoon of the oil, ½ teaspoon of the salt, and ¼ teaspoon of the pepper and toss to coat. Pat the tuna steaks dry with paper towels and then sprinkle the remaining 1 teaspoon salt and ½ teaspoon pepper evenly over all sides. Set aside.

3. When the wheat berries are done, drain them and return them to the pan. Depending on how salty your stock is, you may want to add some salt to the wheat berries, so taste them. Cover again and keep warm.

4. Heat a large skillet over medium-high heat and add the potatoes. Cook until they are golden brown on one side, 4 to 5 minutes. At the same time, heat the remaining 1 tablespoon oil in a second large skillet over high heat; you want it to be nearly smoking.

5. Turn the potatoes over and cook the second side until golden brown, 4 to 5 minutes. At the same time, add the tuna to the second skillet and cook for 1 to 2 minutes on each side; you want the tuna to be raw on the inside, so don't cook it for any longer. Remove the skillet with the potatoes from the heat. Transfer the tuna to a cutting board and cut it into ½-inch-thick slices, each 2- to 3-inches long.

6. To serve, divide the wheat berries equally among four dinner plates. Arrange the tuna and potatoes on top, alternating them as you place them in a row across each serving. Pour ½ cup Garden-Fresh Tomato Sauce over each serving and scatter a bit of chopped basil on top.

Keep It Simple

• You want nice large potatoes. If the Yukon gold potatoes at your store are on the smaller side (or you can't find them) use an Idaho potato instead.

• The Garden-Fresh Tomato Sauce is a killer! But if it's not the season for ripe, juicy tomatoes, or you're in a hurry, a good-quality jarred sauce works great.

• Wheat berries are amazing, but if you're looking for something that cooks faster, try quinoa, farro, barley, or rice.

• Substitute swordfish for the tuna. Or go in a different direction and use steak or chicken instead. All variations are great!

50/50

For every portion you want to make vegetarian, omit 4 ounces of tuna and add an extra half potato (3 more slices). You could also replace the tuna with seared tempeh.

Garden-Fresh Tomato Sauce

MAKES ABOUT 2 CUPS SAUCE

500↓

This sauce is really best when tomatoes are in season. However, I have tried it with quality tomatoes from the store and had good results. Just make sure the tomatoes you start with are as fresh and ripe as possible. You can use this sauce with my Potatoes, Tuna + Wheat Berries (page 219), my Three-Cheese Zucchini Involtini (page 247), or my Zucchini Crust Pizza (page 141), over pasta, on a chicken Parm, draped over a baked potato, or simply soaked up with a piece of crusty bread.

⅓ cup olive oil

4 garlic cloves, sliced

1 small yellow onion, finely chopped

6 cups coarsely chopped ripe tomatoes (6 medium/
    large tomatoes)

1½ teaspoons kosher salt

2 tablespoons chopped fresh basil leaves,
    plus more for serving

1. Heat the oil in a large saucepan over medium-low heat. Stir in the garlic and cook until it is very soft and fragrant, but not browned, 7 to 10 minutes. If the garlic starts to brown, reduce the heat to low.

2. Increase the heat to medium, stir in the onion, and cook until soft and translucent, 5 to 7 minutes.

3. Stir in the tomatoes and salt and mix well. Cook the mixture until most of the liquid has evaporated and it is slightly darker in color, about 30 minutes. Stir in the basil and continue to cook until the sauce has thickened, about 10 minutes more.

4. Serve hot according to your specific recipe directions, scattering extra basil over the top if you like. If there is extra sauce, freeze it in ice cube trays for a handy preportioned ingredient to use later.

Tiny Chicken Meatballs

MAKES 20 SMALL CHICKEN MEATBALLS

500↓

Being the youngest, my brother, EJ, was always the smallest kid in our family; that is until one day he shot up like a bean pole, putting all of us sisters to shame even in our highest heels. But just because he was small did not mean he was quiet, and he could often be seen jumping around the house like a spooked cat. Like my brother, these tiny chicken meatballs may be small, but they pack a big punch, and the size is perfect for folding into casseroles, topping a slice of pizza, or having as an appetizer. Sometimes good things come in tiny packages. I find so many uses for these chicken meatballs; sometimes I make up a big batch and freeze them for future use. You can double, triple, or even quadruple the recipe; just cook them in batches of 20. These meatballs can also be baked for a lighter version, however the color will not be as good.

¼ pound ground chicken

3 tablespoons Basil Pesto (see page 163)

¼ teaspoon kosher salt

1 tablespoon olive oil

1. Combine the chicken, pesto, and salt in a large bowl and mix just until combined; avoid overmixing. Pinch a teaspoon-size amount between your fingers and roll it into a ball; repeat to make 20 meatballs.

2. Heat the oil in a large skillet over medium-high heat. Add the meatballs in a single layer and cook until browned on the bottoms, about 2 minutes. Turn them over and cook until the opposite sides are browned and the meatballs are cooked through, 2 to 3 minutes more. Transfer the meatballs to a paper towel–lined plate to drain.

Beets + Scallops
with Red Onion Jam

MAKES 4 SERVINGS; ABOUT 1¾ CUPS JAM

———————

50/50

I love a good shortcut—unless the shortcut means my husband taking a road in Italy that is seri-ously nowhere on the map—but an ingredient shortcut that adds big flavor to a dish and makes anything taste incredible?! Yes, please! Having this Red Onion Jam on hand means you have many delicious dinners ahead of you. It's great on beets and scallops, giving them the perfect sweetness, and it's also the key to my Fennel + Red Onion Jam Puff Pizza (page 134). Don't stop there, you can spread it on sandwiches, pair it with cheese in an omelet, top chicken, pork, or steak with it, or, as my mother-in-law smartly pointed out, just eat it on a cracker!

Red Onion Jam

2 tablespoons olive oil

2 pounds red onions, thinly sliced

1½ teaspoons kosher salt

6 tablespoons red wine vinegar

3 tablespoons bourbon (optional)

¼ cup honey

1 heaping tablespoon minced fresh thyme leaves

Finely grated zest of 1 lemon

Beets + Scallops

12 small beets (about 1¼ pounds)

3 teaspoons kosher salt

½ teaspoon ground black pepper

2 cups orzo

4 tablespoons (½ stick) unsalted butter, cut into pieces

1 cup thinly sliced scallions, plus more for garnish

2 tablespoons olive oil

12 sea scallops

Red Onion Jam

1. Heat the oil in a large skillet over medium-high heat. Stir in the onions and salt and cook until tender, about 10 minutes.

2. Reduce the heat to medium and stir in the vinegar and the bourbon, if using. Cook until the liquid has reduced by half, 2 to 3 minutes. Stir in the honey, thyme, and lemon zest until incorporated and then cook until the mixture has thickened like jam, about 5 minutes more. (You don't want it to brown, so turn the heat down again if necessary.)

Beets + Scallops

1. Preheat the oven to 375°F.

2. Trim any leaves and roots from the beets. Wrap the beets, all together, in aluminum foil. When the oven is hot, bake them until they can be easily pierced by a fork, 30 to 45 minutes. Leave the oven on, but reduce the oven temperature to 200°F. While the beets are still hot, remove their skins by rubbing with paper towels; the skins should slide off easily. Cut off the top and bottom of each beet so that it becomes the size and shape of a sea scallop; sprinkle with 1 teaspoon of the salt and ¼ teaspoon of the pepper and set aside.

3. Bring a large pot of salted water to a boil, add the orzo and cook according to the package directions until al dente. Drain the orzo and return it to the pot. Add the butter and stir until it has melted; then stir in the scallions and 1 teaspoon of the salt. Cover and keep warm while you prepare the scallops and beets.

4. Pat the scallops dry with paper towels. Sprinkle them with the remaining 1 teaspoon salt and ¼ teaspoon pepper. Heat the oil in a large skillet over high heat. When the oil is shimmering and almost smoking, add the scallops in a single layer and cook until they are golden brown and just cooked through, about 2 minutes per side. Transfer the scallops to a plate and place in the oven to keep warm. Reduce the heat under the skillet to medium, add the beets, and cook until browned and warmed through, 3 minutes per side.

5. To serve, divide the orzo equally among four dinner plates. Place 3 beets and 3 scallops on each serving. Spoon the Red Onion Jam evenly over the scallops and beets, and scatter some chopped scallions over the top.

50/50

- This dish has 3 beets and 3 scallops per serving, so for every portion you want to make vegetarian, add 3 more beets and omit 3 scallops. If that's too many beets for you, try a combo of beets, carrots, and parsnips. Give the carrots or parsnips extra time in the pan in step 4, as they won't be precooked like the beets.
- If I'm doing this recipe with no scallops at all, I also like to add a little arugula to the plate; its peppery finish is a nice contrast to the sweetness of the jam and adds another layer of flavor to this nonmeat version.

Collard Greens Pot Pies

MAKES 4 SERVINGS

FF

You already have a favorite pot pie recipe? OK, but mine is better. Yours was passed down for generations? Oh, that's sweet . . . but mine is still better. Why? Because mine is stuffed with collard greens, of course! This slightly bitter, hearty green breaks up the richness of the traditional dish but leaves the classic pot pie flavor as the star. And best of all, you'll leave your meal feeling great when you think about the massive amount of greens you just ate. The bottom line is, I win for best pot pie and, if you make this your new favorite pot pie recipe, then you'll be a winner too.

2 tablespoons olive oil

1 pound boneless, skinless chicken breast halves

2 teaspoons kosher salt

1 teaspoon ground black pepper

4 tablespoons (½ stick) unsalted butter

1 cup coarsely chopped celery

1 cup coarsely chopped carrots

1 cup coarsely chopped yellow onions

½ cup dry white wine

1 pound collard greens (8 to 10 leaves), coarsely chopped

¼ teaspoon ground nutmeg

6 tablespoons all-purpose flour

3 cups chicken stock

2 cups milk

⅓ cup chopped fresh flat-leaf parsley

Two 9-inch pie crusts (not baked)

1 large egg

1 tablespoon water

¼ cup grated Parmesan cheese (1 ounce)

1. Heat the oil in a large saucepan over high heat. Sprinkle the chicken on all sides with 1 teaspoon of the salt and ½ teaspoon of the pepper. Add the chicken to the pan and cook, turning once, until browned on both sides and cooked through, 10 to 12 minutes. Transfer the chicken to a plate and set aside to rest.

2. Reduce the heat to medium, add the butter to the pan, and cook until melted. Stir in the celery, carrots, onions, and remaining 1 teaspoon salt and cook until the vegetables are soft and tender, 5 to 7 minutes.

3. Stir the wine into the vegetable mixture, scraping any brown bits stuck to the bottom of the pan with your spoon to release them. Cook for a few minutes until most of the wine has evaporated, then stir in the collards and nutmeg. Cook until the collards are wilted and soft, 3 minutes.

4. Preheat the oven to 425°F. Add the flour to the pan with the vegetables and stir to combine well. Cook for 2 minutes. Whisk in the stock and milk and bring the liquid to a simmer. Continue to simmer until the mixture thickens, about 3 minutes. Meanwhile, chop the chicken into bite-size pieces. Add the chicken and parsley to the thickened vegetable mixture and stir to combine.

5. Spoon the vegetable mixture into four 3½-inch oven-safe bowls (like a French onion soup bowl), dividing it equally. Lay the 9-inch pie crusts on a work surface and then, from each crust, cut 2 rounds sized to fit generously over the pot pie bowls. Place a crust on each bowl and crimp it to the edge. Whisk the egg and water in a small bowl and then brush this wash over each crust. Sprinkle the Parmesan evenly over the tops, reserving a bit to add before serving if you wish. Using a small sharp knife, cut a couple of slits in the top of each pot pie. Bake the pot pies until the crusts are brown, about 30 minutes. Dust with the reserved Parmesan and serve.

Keep It simple

- The white wine can easily be replaced with chicken stock or even water.
- The nutmeg gives the dish a special, but subtle, flavor and really complements the greens, but you can leave it out if you don't have it on hand.
- You can bake this dish in 1 or 2 large casseroles (or deep-dish pie plates) instead of in individual bowls. If you need to, be creative and piece the pie crusts to cover! It's finished baking when the crust is brown and the filling is bubbling.
- Make this an under-500 calorie meal by baking or poaching your chicken with no oil, and using a reduced-fat milk instead of whole. It will all still be creamy and delicious and you won't feel as bad about having seconds (or thirds in the case of my husband).
- Make it ahead! Once you have put the crust on, stop! Cover the pot pies with aluminum foil and freeze for up to 2 months. When you're ready to dig in, preheat your oven to 400°F and put the pot pies in with the foil still on. Bake for 40 minutes, remove the foil, and then add the egg wash and Parmesan and bake for 20 to 40 minutes more depending on the size of your dish. (If you don't have freezer-to-oven casseroles, use disposable pans.)

Spaghetti Squash Stuffed
with Mozzarella + Tiny Chicken Meatballs

MAKES 4 SERVINGS

Our friends Brent and Mary are probably the nicest people I've ever met; they are constantly helping us out and also making us laugh, which is sometimes most important. So when they come for dinner it has to be good! Recently, Brent was looking to eat low-carb, so I wanted to serve the Italian comfort food he loves but without any pasta. I knew there is only one solution: spaghetti squash! That night, glass of Bordeaux in hand, I roasted the squash while I whipped up some meatballs and defrosted some homemade sauce, and then married it all together with a little cheese on top. How can a low-carb dinner be this easy and THIS good?! It just might be magic. Prepare to be in love.

2 small spaghetti squash (about 6-inches long, 1.5–2 pounds each)

2 tablespoons olive oil

2½ teaspoons kosher salt

2 cups Nikki's Classic Tomato Sauce (page 172)

8 ounces fresh mozzarella, cut into ½-inch cubes

20 Tiny Chicken Meatballs (page 223)

1 cup grated Parmesan cheese (4 ounces)

Chopped fresh basil leaves, for garnish

1. Preheat the oven to 400°F.

2. Cut the squash in half lengthwise. Using a soupspoon, scoop out the seeds and discard them. Arrange the squash, cut side up, on a rimmed baking sheet. Drizzle the oil evenly over each piece and then sprinkle with the salt; this may seem like a lot but the salt will seep into the deeper parts of the squash as it cooks. Bake the squash until the flesh is tender and can be easily separated with the tines of a fork, 35 to 40 minutes.

3. While the squash bake, if you haven't already done so, make the chicken meatballs. When the squash are done, transfer the baking sheet to a wire rack to cool; leave the oven on.

4. When the squash are cool enough to handle, use a dinner fork to gently separate the flesh into spaghetti-like strands and transfer them to a large bowl; take care not to rip the shell, as you are going to stuff it. Add the tomato sauce and mozzarella to the bowl and toss until the filling is combined.

5. Spoon or fork the filling back into the squash shells, dividing it equally. Arrange 5 meatballs on each piece and then spoon a scant ¼ cup Parmesan evenly over each, reserving a little Parmesan for garnish. Return the squash to the baking sheet and to the oven and bake until the cheese has melted and slightly browned, about 20 minutes. Scatter the basil and reserved Parmesan over the tops and serve.

Keep It Simple

- There are more and more good jarred tomato sauces available. And although I think my tomato sauce is still the cream of the crop, using a store-bought sauce can make this recipe prep fly by. The same thing goes for the pesto in my mini chicken meatballs!
- To cut the prep time dramatically, cook the squash in the microwave instead of baking them: Simply put the seeded halves, cut side down, in a shallow microwavable container with ½ cup water. Cook on high for 5 to 10 minutes depending on the size of the squash. Scoop out the flesh and toss with oil and salt as directed in step 2.
- You can prep this ahead of time: Complete the recipe up to the point where the squash are filled and ready to bake; then refrigerate them. Later, just pull them out and bake at 400°F for 40 to 60 minutes.

FF

Don't stuff the squash shells, but instead mix the strands, sauce, and mozzarella together and spoon into a casserole dish. Cover with Parmesan cheese and broil. No need to show the squash-leery exactly where their dinner came from; it can be our little secret. This is also a great way to go if you can't find the right size squash for individual portions. With this method it doesn't matter if you get 2 small squash or 1 big one.

Sweet Potato Pie
Topped with Pears,
Blue Cheese + Skirt Steak

MAKES 2 SERVINGS; DOUBLE THE RECIPE AS YOU WISH

FF | 50/50

When I'm developing a recipe, I may look like I'm just staring. What I'm really doing is thinking—about how each flavor will work with all the others, about the specific ingredients and techniques needed to pull it together. This sweet potato pie is about bringing all the pieces together. You have to cook the pie and the steak simultaneously so that both are ready at the same time. You want just the right chunks of blue cheese—taken from a block—to give a satisfying blue bite atop contrasting sweetness below. And a touch of lemon is the perfect thing to keep the vibrant pear from turning brown. So no, I'm not just staring, I'm creating masterpieces, and sometimes I'm thinking about kittens, but mostly it's creating masterpieces.

½ pound skirt steak, at room temperature

3 tablespoons plus 2 teaspoons olive oil

2 teaspoons kosher salt, plus more as needed

¼ teaspoon ground black pepper, plus more as needed

1 large sweet potato, peeled and grated (about 4 cups)

1 leek, white and light green parts only, thinly sliced crosswise

2 garlic cloves, minced

¼ teaspoon ground cinnamon

⅛ teaspoon ground nutmeg

2 large eggs

¼ cup all-purpose flour

½ cup balsamic vinegar

½ Bartlett pear

Juice of ½ lemon

1 cup trimmed watercress sprigs

2 ounces blue cheese, crumbled (about ½ cup)

1. Drizzle the steak with ½ teaspoon of the oil and sprinkle with ¼ teaspoon salt and ⅛ teaspoon pepper; turn it over and do the same on the other side.

2. In a large bowl, combine the sweet potatoes, leeks, garlic, 1½ teaspoons salt, and the cinnamon and nutmeg. Add the eggs and stir to combine. Add the flour and stir until everything is well mixed.

3. Heat a small saucepan over medium-low heat, add the vinegar and cook until it has reduced by two-thirds and is thick and syrupy, 7 to 10 minutes. Keep an eye on the balsamic syrup as it can burn easily. Meanwhile, core the pear and cut it lengthwise into thin slices. Put the slices in a medium bowl, add the lemon juice, and stir gently to coat.

4. Heat an 8-inch nonstick skillet over medium heat. Add 2 tablespoons of the oil to the skillet and then, using a spatula, spread out the sweet potato mixture in an even layer over the bottom. Flatten the top and cook until the underside is golden brown, about 5 minutes. Loosen the sides with the spatula and invert a plate over the skillet. Using oven mitts, flip the skillet and plate to transfer the potato pie onto the plate. Add 1 more tablespoon of oil to the skillet and, keeping the cooked side up, slide the potato pie back into the skillet. Continue to cook until the underside is golden brown, about 5 minutes more.

5. At the same time, preheat a grill pan over high heat. Add the steak and cook until medium-rare, 5 minutes per side, or to your desired doneness. Let the steak rest for at least 3 minutes; slice against the grain into thin strips.

6. While the steak is resting, add the watercress, remaining 1 teaspoon oil, and a pinch each of salt and pepper to the bowl with the pear slices; toss gently to coat with the lemon juice.

7. Transfer the potato pie to a serving plate. Arrange the steak, pears, and watercress on top, scatter with the blue cheese, and drizzle with the balsamic syrup. Cut into wedges and serve.

Keep It Simple
- You can substitute an apple for the pear and leave out the nutmeg and cinnamon if desired.
- You can use any type of blue cheese or pear in this recipe, and feel free to replace the watercress with romaine, green leaf, or whatever variety of lettuce you have on hand.
- Instead of making the balsamic syrup you can find reduced balsamic, sometimes called balsamic drizzle at some larger grocery stores.

FF
What kid wouldn't like steak and potatoes—even if he has to fight through a little salad to get there? But it's probably best to omit the blue cheese when serving this to your kids; or try replacing it with dollops of cream cheese or goat cheese.

50/50
- To make the pie half vegetarian, use only 4 ounces of steak and add an extra 1 cup of watercress to the recipe. Mound the steak over half of the pie and the extra salad over the other.
- Or for a completely vegetarian version, totally omit the steak, and add an extra 1 cup of watercress and use a whole pear.

Nacho Risotto
with Butternut Squash

MAKES 4 SERVINGS

———

50/50

Let's have some fun!! Just because a meal is elegant in flavor and full of veggies doesn't mean it can't be fun, and this nacho risotto is literally a good time on a plate. I've taken all the things you love about nachos and twisted them into a meal that is entertaining worthy. The cheese of the nachos has become a cheesy risotto made richer and sweeter with tons of butternut squash; added on are your remaining usual toppings, spiced beef, pickled jalapeños, and tomatoes, and let's not forget the chips! If you're not having fun now there is something wrong with you. Seriously, see a doctor because I'm having a blast.

1 small butternut squash (2 pounds)

4 tablespoons olive oil

3 teaspoons kosher salt

4 cups chicken stock

1 cup water

1 medium yellow onion, finely chopped

4 garlic cloves, minced

1½ cups Arborio rice

1 pound ground beef

1½ teaspoons ancho or chipotle chili powder

2 large tomatoes, coarsely chopped

2 tablespoons finely chopped fresh cilantro

Juice of 1 lime

2 cups shredded sharp cheddar cheese

½ cup grated Parmesan cheese (2 ounces)

16 pickled jalapeño chile slices

4 tablespoons sour cream

12 tortilla chips

1. Preheat the oven to 400°F.

2. Peel the squash and cut it in half lengthwise. Using a soupspoon, scoop out the seeds and discard them. Cut the squash into ½-inch-thick slices and then into ½-inch chunks; you should have about 3 cups of chunks. Put the chunks in a medium bowl and add 1 tablespoon of the oil and ½ teaspoon of the salt and toss to coat. Spread the squash out on a rimmed baking sheet and bake in the preheated oven until tender, about 30 minutes.

3. Transfer the squash to a food processor or blender. Process to a smooth puree, adding ½ cup water if the result is especially stiff; you should have about 1½ cups puree. Set aside.

4. To start the risotto, pour the stock and 1 cup water into a medium saucepan over low heat. Briefly heat the remaining 3 tablespoons oil in a large saucepan over medium heat and stir in the onion and garlic. Cook until tender and translucent, 5 to 7 minutes. Stir the rice into the onion and garlic, and cook, stirring occasionally, until it is slightly toasted, 5 to 7 minutes more.

5. Add 1 cup of the now-warm stock (a measuring ladle is a great help here) and stir vigorously until the rice has absorbed all the liquid. Add another cup of stock and continue to stir until it has been absorbed by the rice. Stir in the squash puree and mix well.

6. Continue in this way, adding stock 1 cup at a time and stirring constantly until the liquid has been absorbed before adding more, until the rice is tender but still has a slight bite. Add only as much stock as you need; you may not need it all and, should you need more, just add some simmering water).

7. When the risotto is almost done, heat a large skillet over medium-high heat and add the beef, 1 teaspoon of the salt, and the chili powder. Stir together, breaking up the meat, and cook until the meat has browned and is no longer pink, about 5 minutes. Meanwhile, mix the tomatoes, cilantro, lime juice, and ½ teaspoon of the salt in a small bowl.

8. Stir the cheddar and Parmesan cheeses into the risotto. Taste, and add up to 1 teaspoon of the remaining salt as you wish; the amount will vary depending on how salty your cheese and stock are.

9. To serve, divide the risotto equally among four dinner plates and top each plate with one-quarter of the beef, ¼ cup of the tomato mixture, 4 jalapeño slices, and 1 tablespoon of sour cream; then crumble 3 tortilla chips over each.

Keep It Simple

• Top the cheesy squash risotto with any toppings you like—think about what you love to put on a plate of nachos and run with it.
• Ancho and chipotle chili powders are two of my favorites and can be found at most grocery stores, but you can use regular chili powder, chipotle puree (see Appendix, page 259), or a packet of taco seasoning instead.
• Many grocery stores sell butternut squash already peeled and cubed in the produce section. It can be a great time-saver, just make sure you have about 3 cups worth.
• Replace the tomato mixture with a premade salsa if you prefer.

Sweet + Spicy Stuffed Poblanos

MAKES 6 SERVINGS

500↓ | 50/50

When my sister-in-law Anne comes to town with her delectable children it's always a good time. But when those sweet bundles of energy go to bed, it's time for the adults to go out to enjoy some wine and pasta and catch up. However, someone has to stay behind. Recently, when my mother in-law, Marge, graciously volunteered, I brought her these delicious stuffed poblanos so she could enjoy a nice meal while we were out. The chiles are roasted on the outside, and have soaked up the tangy salsa verde; when you dig in you discover a creamy, cheesy, spicy filling that makes you want to take bite after bite. You don't need to go out; with these the restaurant meal is right on your table.

2 medium sweet potatoes

2 links chorizo (4 ounces each)

1 tablespoon olive oil

2 cubanelle peppers or green bell peppers, seeded and coarsely chopped

1 medium yellow onion, coarsely chopped

4 garlic cloves, minced

2 teaspoons kosher salt

1 teaspoon ground cumin

4 ounces Manchego cheese, cut into ¼-inch cubes

6 large poblano chiles

One 16-ounce jar salsa verde

Cooked rice, for serving (optional)

Queso fresco or sour cream, for serving

1. Preheat the oven to 400°F. Poke several holes in each sweet potato with fork.

2. Cook the potatoes in the microwave on high for 5 minutes; turn them over and microwave again until soft, 2 to 5 minutes more.

3. Place a small skillet over medium heat. Remove the casings from the chorizo and crumble the meat into the pan. Cook for about 4 minutes; breaking it apart with a spoon as it cooks until you have ¼- to ½-inch pieces. Reduce the heat to low and cook 2 minutes more.

4. Heat the oil in a large skillet over medium heat. Stir in the cubanelles, onion, garlic, salt, and cumin and cook until the vegetables are tender, 5 to 7 minutes.

5. Remove the vegetable mixture from the heat. Cut the sweet potatoes in half and scoop their flesh into the vegetables, stirring and mashing to combine. To complete the filling, fold in the chorizo and then the Manchego cheese.

6. Spread a little salsa verde over the bottom of a 9 × 13-inch baking dish. Cut off the top of each poblano and remove as many of the seeds and ribs as possible or cut the poblanos down the side and keep the top intact as shown. Stuff the poblanos with the filling and arrange them in the dish, tucking the top of the chile back onto each one. Spoon the rest of the salsa verde evenly over the poblanos. Cover the dish and bake until the poblanos are tender, 45 to 60 minutes, basting twice with the salsa verde. Serve immediately, over cooked rice if you wish, topped with a little crumbled queso fresco or sour cream.

Keep It Simple
• Poblanos have a great flavor and just a little heat, but if you can't find them take a green or red bell pepper, cut it in half lengthwise and scoop out the seeds and ribs, then stuff and cook cut side up.
• Limited pantry? Replace the Manchego with cheddar or parmesan, sub the chorizo for any spicy sausage and use regular salsa or enchilada sauce instead of the salsa verde.

50/50
You use about 2 oz or half a chorizo link per person in this recipe, so simply cook up 2 oz less chorizo per person for whomever wants theirs vegetarian. No need to add anything else.

Tomato-Fennel Ragu + Baked Eggs

MAKES 4 SERVINGS

500↓ | 50/50

When life gets too busy and my plate gets too full I take seemingly less important things off it. Things like yoga, walks, reality TV, and lunch with friends fall by the wayside. But I have learned from my friend Michelle that there needs to be balance. No matter how hectic her life she will always make time to meet for coffee. So though I thought I had "more important things to do," I had Michelle over for lunch and served Tomato-Fennel Ragu + Baked Eggs—flavorful, comforting, yet perfectly light. Michelle feels time spent like this is as important as anything else, and I realize how right she is. It's all about balance. Luckily, if I sometimes find myself way out of balance and about to fall, I have great friends like her to catch me.

3 tablespoons olive oil

1 fennel bulb (about 1 pound), halved and then thinly sliced, a few fronds reserved

1 Vidalia onion, thinly sliced

5 garlic cloves, thinly sliced

4 teaspoons kosher salt

¼ cup tomato paste

Two 28-ounce cans crushed tomatoes

Two chorizo links (4 ounces each)

¼ cup chopped fresh basil leaves, plus more for garnish

2 tablespoons chopped fresh mint leaves

½ teaspoon crushed red pepper flakes

Finely grated zest of 1 lemon

4 (or 8) large eggs (depending on your appetite!)

Sliced crusty white bread, for serving

1. Heat the oil in a large, deep skillet over medium heat. Stir in the sliced fennel, onion, garlic, and 2 teaspoons of the salt and cook until the vegetables are tender and translucent, about 7 minutes.

2. Add the tomato paste to the skillet, stir to incorporate, and cook for 2 to 3 minutes more. Then stir in the crushed tomatoes and the remaining 2 teaspoons salt and cook until thickened and reduced by about one-third, 15 to 20 minutes.

3. While the tomatoes cook, heat a small skillet over medium-low heat. Add the chorizo links, cover, and cook until they are cooked through, about 12 minutes. Chop the links into ½-inch pieces and set aside.

4. Reduce the heat under the tomato sauce to medium-low. Stir in the basil, mint, red pepper flakes, and lemon zest. Make 4 wells in the sauce and gently crack 1 (or 2) eggs into each. Cover the pan (use aluminum foil if your pan doesn't have a lid) and cook until the whites of the eggs are set and the yolks are runny, 7 to 9 minutes. Cook longer if you prefer firm yolks.

5. To serve, spoon 1 (or 2) eggs and some sauce onto each of four dinner plates. Divide the chorizo equally over each and then scatter the reserved fennel fronds on top. Add some bread and serve, suggesting to everyone they dip the bread into the eggs and sauce. Pass more sauce at the table if people are having a good time with the dipping!

Keep It Simple
- You can use any type of sausage you like instead of the chorizo. Or if you prefer, add cooked and crumbled bacon instead.
- The mint and the basil together really make this dish shine, but it would be super tasty with just one of them, or whatever your favorite herb is.
- Depending on how much dipping you do, you may end up with extra sauce—which is a good problem to have. Use this sauce anywhere you would use tomato sauce, or freeze it and defrost it for the next time you want to make this dish.

50/50
You've got eggs, a hearty tomato and fennel sauce, and crusty bread. You don't need the sausage (especially if you prepare 2 eggs per serving), so just leave it off any plates you want to be meat-free.

Kale Crepes
with Sweet Potato–Cream Cheese

MAKES 4 TO 5 FILLED CREPES

500↓ | FF | Make It Meaty

Although as a kid green things scared me, somehow, over many years, this prejudice changed. I now view green things as interesting, intriguing, and tasty. Kale is one of my favorite greens, for both its crazy awesome nutrition (Vitamins A, C, K, calcium, and protein anyone?) and its sturdy texture. And one day it found its way into my crepe batter, turning it into this gorgeous green showstopper. For this recipe you can use any kale you have in the crisper drawer: dinosaur, curly, wild garden kale, whatever. And since the crepe is filled with a sweet potato–cream cheese, I'd like to think even nine-year-old Nikki might give it a try . . . yeah, probably not, but you get my drift.

Kale Crepes

½ cup packed kale leaves

½ cup all-purpose flour

1 extra-large egg

¼ cup whole milk

¼ cup water

1 tablespoon honey

⅛ teaspoon kosher salt

2 tablespoons unsalted butter, plus more if needed

Filling + Toppings

¼ cup olive oil

4 medium sweet potatoes, peeled and chopped into ¼-inch dice

2 medium yellow onions, coarsely chopped

6 garlic cloves, sliced

2 teaspoons kosher salt

4 ounces cream cheese

½ cup coarsely chopped hazelnuts

Kale Crepes

1. To make the batter, add the kale, flour, egg, milk, water, honey, and salt to a blender and process until the mixture is smooth and the kale is completely pureed.

2. Preheat the oven to 200°F.

3. Melt ½ tablespoon of the butter in an 8-inch, nonstick skillet or crepe pan over medium-low heat. Add ¼ cup of the batter and, working quickly, tilt the pan in all directions to coat the bottom. Cook until the underside of the crepe is set and slightly browned in spots, about 2 minutes. Using a spatula, flip the crepe over and then cook the opposite side until it, too, is slightly brown, about 1½ minutes. Transfer the crepe to a plate and repeat the process with the remaining batter and butter. Place the plate with the crepes in the oven to keep warm while you make the Filling + Topping (below).

4. When the filling and toppings are ready to use, arrange the crepes on a work surface. Spoon ⅓ cup of the filling along the center of each crepe and then roll it up to enclose the filling. Serve the crepes immediately, topped with the reserved sautéed sweet potato mixture and sprinkled with the hazelnuts.

Filling + Topping

1. Heat the oil in a large skillet over medium heat. Add the sweet potatoes, onions, garlic, and salt and cook until tender and browned, 7 to 10 minutes.

2. To make the filling, transfer half the potato mixture to a clean food processer or blender; cover the remainder and keep warm to use as the topping. Add the cream cheese to the food processor and process until the filling is smooth.

FF

If green things scare your kids, leave the kale out of the batter for a more familiar pancake-looking crepe and instead, chop the kale up finely and mix it into the sweet potato-cream cheese— same ingredients, fewer fights at the dinner table.

Make It Meaty

I find this dish to be very filling, but if you just have to have a little meat, try cooked sausage, ground turkey, or even leftover meat loaf folded into the filling.

Three-Cheese Zucchini Involtini in Summer Tomato Sauce

MAKES 8 INVOLTINI; SERVES 4

500↓ | FF

My father is Italian, granted only 50 percent, but he likes to think of himself as a full-fledged Italian man. Though that only makes me 25 percent Italian (and mostly German), when it comes to my food, my Italian heritage definitely beat out my German roots for title of Nikki's favorite cuisine. Give me pasta over Wiener schnitzel any day of the week. Italian flavors are what I come back to time and time again, and these involtini are everything you could want from an Italian meal, with some extra twists of lemon, mint, and grilled zucchini that make the dish truly dance. My father is obviously so proud.

2 large zucchini

8 ounces ricotta cheese

8 ounces fresh mozzarella, cut to ½-inch cubes

2 ounces Parmesan cheese, cut to ¼-inch cubes

¼ cup chopped fresh basil leaves

1 large egg

1 teaspoon kosher salt

1 tablespoon olive oil

¼ teaspoon ground black pepper

2 cups Garden-Fresh Tomato Sauce (page 222) or Nikki's Classic Tomato Sauce (page 172)

2 tablespoons chopped fresh mint leaves

Finely grated zest of 1 lemon

1. Preheat the oven to 450°F. Preheat a gas or charcoal grill, to medium-high if you have that option (or plan to use a grill pan). Cut each zucchini lengthwise into four ¼-inch-thick strips.

2. Put the ricotta, mozzarella, Parmesan, basil, egg, and ½ teaspoon of the salt in a large bowl and mix well. Cover and refrigerate.

3. If using a grill pan, preheat it over medium-high heat. Mix the oil, the remaining ½ teaspoon salt, and the pepper on a plate. Brush the mixture over both sides of each zucchini strip, resting the strips on the plate until all are coated. Arrange the zucchini on the grill or grill pan and cook until the strips are soft but not mushy, about 5 minutes, turning once (stop cooking them as soon as you are able to bend them at a 90-degree angle without breaking). Return them to the plate and set aside to cool slightly.

4. Remove the cheese mixture from the refrigerator. Mix the tomato sauce with the mint and lemon zest in a small bowl. Spread ½ cup of this mixture in the bottom of a medium baking dish (11 × 7-inch or equivalent).

5. Make the involtini one at a time: Roll a bit of the cheese mixture between your palms—you want it to be about the size of a golf ball—and place it on one end of a zucchini strip. Roll the strip up over the filling, rolling it all the way to the end, and place it in the baking dish. When all 8 involtini are arranged in the dish, spread the rest of the tomato sauce over them and place the dish in the oven. Bake until the sauce is bubbling and the cheese is beginning to brown, about 40 minutes. Serve hot!

Keep It Simple

- Though my Classic Tomato Sauce and Garden-Fresh Tomato Sauce recipes are quite simply AMAZING, you can of course use your favorite store-bought sauce.
- The zucchini can also be replaced with yellow squash or eggplant.
- I like using chunks of mozzarella and Parmesan in the filling because they make each bite taste a little different and give the dish an addictive quality that keeps you going back for more. However, shredded mozzarella and Parmesan work very well instead and, if you buy them that way, can really help speed up the prep time for this dish.

FF

The Garden-Fresh Tomato Sauce looks a little rustic. Going with my Classic Tomato Sauce recipe or a bottled sauce can make this dish look more familiar, more like the traditional Italian food your kids may be used to.

Make It Meaty

- Add meat to this dish by serving it with my Tiny Chicken Meatballs (page 223) or Breaded Chicken (see page 152) or even some seared scallops.
- Or you can add a little meaty kick by placing a strip of prosciutto on the zucchini before filling and rolling it up. Yum.

Tomato Parm
with Eggplant Sauce

MAKES 4 SERVINGS

FF | Make It Meaty

We have all heard of Eggplant Parm with Tomato Sauce, but today, we're getting crazy, today we are mixing everything up and making . . . wait for it . . . it's going to be good . . . Tomato Parm with Eggplant Sauce! See what I did there?! It's a juicy fresh tomato, breaded, so it soaks up the eggplant sauce while staying crisp, and then smothered in cheese. This is comfort food taken up a notch.

⅓ cup all-purpose flour

2 large eggs

2 tablespoons water

1 cup dry bread crumbs

1 teaspoon kosher salt

¼ teaspoon ground black pepper

¼ teaspoon garlic powder

Eight 1-inch-thick slices tomato (from 4 large firm tomatoes)

¼ cup olive oil

1 cup Eggplant Sauce (page 158)

2 cups shredded mozzarella

2 medium tomatoes, finely chopped

¼ cup finely chopped fresh basil leaves

1. Put the flour on a small plate. Whisk together the eggs and water in a shallow bowl. Mix the bread crumbs, ½ teaspoon salt, pepper, and garlic powder on a second small plate. Toss the tomato slices with the remaining salt.

2. One at a time, dip each tomato slice first into the flour, turning to dust both sides and tapping off any excess; then into the egg mixture, turning to coat both sides and allowing any excess to drip off; and finally into the bread crumbs, making sure the crumbs coat all sides of the slice. Lay the coated slices on a clean dry surface.

3. Heat the oil in a large skillet over medium-high heat. Add the tomato slices in a single layer (working in batches if they don't all fit at once) and cook until golden brown on both sides, 1 to 2 minutes per side. Transfer the slices to a paper towel–lined plate to drain.

4. Turn on the broiler. Arrange the tomato slices on a rimmed baking sheet. Top each slice with 2 tablespoons Eggplant Sauce and ¼ cup mozzarella. Place under the broiler until the cheese has melted and slightly browned, 3 to 5 minutes. Transfer to individual plates, dividing the chopped tomatoes and basil equally over each serving.

Keep It Simple

If you're in a rush, skip the breading and frying part of the recipe and simply cover the tomato slices with eggplant sauce and cheese and then broil as instructed. The added bonus—this makes the dish even leaner!

FF

Though there are a lot of veggies in here, they are all presented in a kid-friendly way, as the tomatoes are panfried and covered in cheese and the eggplant sauce just looks like a slightly different tomato sauce. But if your kids are fresh-tomato shy, skip the chopped tomato topping to help hide the fact that they are eating a veggie-filled meal.

Make It Meaty

Replace 2 tomato slices with 2 similar size pieces of thinly sliced chicken breast. Dredge the chicken the same way as you do the tomatoes and cook in the oil until the center of the chicken is no longer pink, 3 to 5 minutes depending on the thickness of the chicken. Top with sauce and cheese and broil until brown.

Root Vegetables

These dirty, dense veggies are like hidden gems that need to be dug out of the earth, cleaned up, and cut (or cooked) in the right way for them to really shine. And shine they will! Many home cooks overlook things like turnips and celeriac (celery root) in the grocery store. And even more people think carrots and beets only belong in salads. But in this book I don't judge any vegetable by how it is "normally" cooked up. I think beets can be made into hummus, celeriac can add a hearty freshness to lobster, and sweet potatoes can shine in soups and be made into crepe fillings. Not to mention that parsnips make great "pasta" and onions create intensely flavorful dips. And the best part about these gems is they are some of the more affordable things in the produce department and, of course, always much more affordable than real gems (though I have a feeling you already knew that).

Recipe List

Afterword

Willa's Lemonade Cheesecakes

MAKES 6 SMALL CHEESECAKES

November 25 is my daughter Willa's birthday. It's the day our amazing, incredible, beautiful, vivacious, perfect, precious little baby was born, all 8 pounds 4 ounces of her. However she was born sleeping. For reasons far beyond our comprehension her heart just stopped. Though we wanted a lifetime of memories with her, we feel lucky to have had her with us for 10 months. In that time she was a TV star, making her first appearance on the finale of Food Network Star. She visited beaches near and far as I worked on my belly tan, and most of the time she was simply my companion, my buddy. Food-wise I always knew what she liked as she made her requests very known to me. Lemonade became something I could not live without, and she sent me searching all over New York City for the perfect ratio of lemons to water. Sugar was request number two: She was on a real Sour Patch Kids kick. And last, let us not forget, the cheese; like mother, like daughter, she loved her cheese. So when I wanted to write a recipe just for her I thought I would take all these things and make her baby Lemonade Cheesecakes. Nothing gives me more joy than cooking for the ones I love, and this one is for my Willa.

Cheesecakes

Two 8-ounce bars cream cheese, at room temperature

½ cup plus ⅓ cup granulated sugar (keep separate)

2 tablespoons cornstarch

6 tablespoons heavy cream, at room temperature (purchase ½ pint)

Finely grated zest and juice of 1 lemon

1½ teaspoons vanilla extract

1 large egg, at room temperature

6 store-bought premade mini graham cracker crusts in foil pans

Topping

10 tablespoons heavy cream (the portion of the ½ pint not used for the cheesecakes)

¾ teaspoon vanilla extract

1½ tablespoons powdered sugar

6 tablespoons granulated sugar

6 yellow Sour Patch Kids

6 very thin strips lemon peel

Cheesecakes

1. Preheat the oven to 350°F. Have ready a baking pan (with sides) large enough to hold the premade crusts in a single layer (use 2 baking pans if you need to).

2. Place 1 bar of the cream cheese, the ⅓ cup granulated sugar, and the cornstarch in a food processor and process until combined and smooth (you can use an electric mixer for this instead, on medium speed). Add the remaining bar of cream cheese and process until well incorporated.

3. Add the 6 tablespoons cream, the remaining ½ cup granulated sugar, the lemon zest, lemon juice, and the vanilla to the cream cheese mixture and pulse to combine. Add the egg and process until the mixture is smooth.

4. Pour the cream cheese mixture into the premade crusts, dividing it equally. Arrange the crusts in the baking pan. Pull out the oven rack, and place the baking pan with the crusts in the oven. Carefully pour hot water into the baking pan to come halfway up the side of the crusts in their pans. Carefully push in the oven rack and bake the cheesecakes until the centers are set, about 20 minutes. Turn off the oven, crack the door open, and leave the cheesecakes in the oven until they are close to room temperature, about 20 minutes. Carefully lift the cooled cheesecakes from the water and transfer them to the refrigerator; chill for at least 1 hour.

Topping

1. While the cheesecakes are chilling, whip the cream, vanilla, and powdered sugar in the bowl of a mixer fitted with a whisk attachment on high speed until soft peaks form, 1 to 2 minutes. Refrigerate the whipped cream, covered, until ready to serve.

2. When ready to serve the cheesecakes, place 1 tablespoon of the granulated sugar on each, spread it around and then tap off any excess. Using a torch, brulee the sugar (melt and brown it); or turn on the broiler and place the cheesecakes under it very briefly. Tip the cheesecakes out of their pans. Place a dollop of whipped cream on each and decorate with a Sour Patch Kid and a strip of lemon peel.

Keep It Simple

• Depending on their size, the cheesecake filling may be more than enough for 6 crusts, and I always buy extra so none of that delicious filling goes to waste. If you end up with 1 or 2 additional cheese-cakes, increase the total granulated sugar amount accordingly, so you can top each with 1 table-spoonful.

• You can also bake extra filling in a muffin tin, for crustless individual servings.

Appendix

Ingredient cutting definitions

Coarsely chopped/chopped. Irregular, roughly ½-inch pieces; these don't need to be consistent in size or perfectly square. When coarsely chopped is called for in my recipes, most of the time the size of the pieces doesn't matter because they will later be pureed in the food processor or the size of the cut is up to your preference.

Finely chopped. The ingredient should be evenly cut into pieces about ¼-inch in size.

Very finely chopped. You want the ingredient cut very small, about ⅛-inch.

Minced. These pieces should be chopped as finely as possible. Minced is usually indicated for garlic and herbs because you need 1 clove of garlic or 1 tablespoon of herbs to be evenly distributed throughout a dish, and little pieces aid in that.

Thinly sliced. Slices should be about a ⅛-inch. I generally cut onions that I'm going to sauté in half lengthwise before slicing them crosswise; this way they have a flat surface to rest on the cutting board while I slice.

Very thinly sliced. Slices should be as thin as possible, less than ⅛ inch. A mandoline can be helpful to achieve this.

Basic prep techniques

Chipotle puree. Chipotle peppers are actually smoked jalapeños. You will find them mixed with an adobo sauce in 7-ounce cans next to the packets of taco seasoning, tortillas, and cans of green chiles. For most recipes you only need a small amount of these peppers with sauce, so put the contents of the can in a food processor or blender, puree until smooth, and transfer to a resealable food storage bag. Use the amount specified in your recipe and store the rest, with the bag standing up, in the freezer. The extra puree will freeze into a log at the bottom of the bag. Once frozen cut off pieces as needed for other recipes.

Lemongrass. To sauté this Asian herb, first peel a layer or two, discard the top half of the stalk, and cut the rest as the recipe states. If you are using the lemongrass to infuse a broth it is always nice to smash the lemongrass with a heavy pan or meat mallet before cutting.

Homemade bread crumbs. There's no problem with going to the store and buying bread crumbs. The problem is that they don't sell big, thick bread crumbs that make the most delectable crunch on top of my Eggplant Pasta Bake with Fresh Mozzarella + Thyme Bread Crumbs (page 160) or Eggplant Fans with Caesar Dressing + Bread Crumbs (page 186), so let's talk about making your own. Since most nights it's just me and my husband at the dinner table, we don't usually (hopefully) finish a whole baguette in a single seating. Even if I use a couple slices for my eggs the next morning, I am often left with a semihard half a loaf of bread. So what I do is break it into chunks and pulse it in the food processor until I get bread

MINCED

FINELY CHOPPED

VERY THINLY SLICED

COARSELY CHOPPED

THINLY SLICED

crumbs. Just transfer them to a resealable bag and store in the freezer. Then pull them straight out of the freezer and top casseroles with them, sauté them in a pan with some butter, or defrost them, which will take only minutes on your counter-top, and use them in your meatballs. Not only are homemade bread crumbs delicious but also you'll be repurposing something that might have ended up in the trash. So these coarse, dry, but not toasted, bread crumbs are the type I mean for you to use when the recipe calls for homemade bread crumbs.

Hard-boiled eggs. Arrange the desired number of large eggs in a single layer in an appropriate-size saucepan and add cold water to cover by 1 inch. Set over high heat and bring to a boil; then cover, remove from the heat, and let sit for 10 minutes. Transfer the eggs to a bowl of ice water and set aside to cool; peel when ready to use.

Roasted peppers. Roasting is a great way to add a subtle smoky flavor to peppers and chiles while gently cooking them. It makes them perfect to eat immediately or to add to pastas, soups, and so much more. The trick to roasting is to simply char/blacken the skin of the pepper (at least 80 percent of the skin) over an open flame or close to a heat source such as a broiler. You can, of course, buy roasted peppers in a jar, but sometimes you'll find that they come packed in oil, adding unnecessary fat and calories and causing the pepper to become extra soft the longer it sits in the jar. So skip the jar and save money by roasting up several peppers when they are inexpensive and in season, then wrap them individually in foil or a resealable food storage bag and pull them out as you need them; they freeze beautifully and will stay good until peppers start popping up again at your farmers' market.

To roast peppers: Using tongs, simply place peppers over the flame on your gas stovetop and cook until they are mostly black on all sides, about 5 minutes, turning as needed. If you don't have a gas stove (or just prefer to use your broiler) you can place them under your broiler, as close to the heat source as possible. Put the blackened peppers in a plastic food storage bag or in a bowl and seal the bag, or cover the bowl with plastic wrap. When the peppers are cool, rub off the skins with paper towels and remove their stems and seeds.

Seeding a pomegranate. The easy and non-messy way to seed a pomegranate is by filling a large bowl with water, cutting the pomegranate into quarters, and submerging the pieces in the water. Then dig your hands in and separate the seeds from the white pith and the seeds will sink to the bottom while the inedible parts float to the top. Or you can simply separate the seeds right onto a plate, but fair warning, you will end up with a seed or five on your floor, you will step on one, and the next day you will find little red dots all over the carpet. You have been warned.

Toasting nuts. Toasting nuts is always a good idea; it brings out their flavor and gives them a richer color. To toast any nut, set a small skillet over low heat. Add the nuts to the dry pan (they have plenty of oil in them naturally, so no need to oil the pan) and cook, stirring occasionally, until golden brown on all sides, about 5 minutes. And remember they can go from perfectly brown to black bits in a flash, or in as long as it takes to get distracted by a 50-percent off e-mail from my favorite store. So don't leave the pan, even for 75-percent off shoes; the shoes will still be there but your nuts will be burned!

Toasting seeds. Winter squash give you a present in the form of their seeds. Instead of automatically sending these to the compost, I like to toast them to use as a tasty, crunchy garnish. Preheat the oven to 400°F. Clean any fibers from the seeds and spread out the seeds on a rimmed baking sheet. Bake until the seeds are brown and crisp, 7 to 10 minutes; then set aside.

Find step-by-step photos of these techniques and others at NikkiDinkiCooking.com.

Nikki's Salt Rant

PLEASE NOTE! In this book the recipes call for kosher salt; the granules of kosher salt are much larger than those of regular table salt. So if you are using regular salt you will want to use about half as much as I recommend and then taste and add more if needed.

As much as I have given you guys some guidelines when it comes to salt in these recipes, it can be very hard to say exactly how much you need. Other ingredients in the recipe such as stock or Parmesan cheese can have varying amounts of salt, making it hard to say how much salt the overall dish will need. For example, say I'm making a soup and when I made the recipe with my chicken stock (which is very salty) I only needed 1 teaspoon of salt, but when you make it with your brand of chicken stock (that is only kind of salty) you may need double the amount of salt. My point is that there are many factors that go into how much salt a dish needs. The best thing you can do is keep on tasting the dish and salt it to your liking.

A wise woman once said "If you have never oversalted a dish than you are probably always undersalting"—Dinki. There is a very fine line between a dish being perfectly salted and over-salted. Considering how thin that line is and how easy it is to cross it, if you have never oversalted something then you are likely always below the line of perfectly salted. Try adding a little more salt than you naturally would the next time you make a dish. You may find that just an extra dash of salt really takes your cooking to the next level.

After all this salt talk you are probably thinking, "Geeze Nikki, you're really into salt, but shouldn't we be limiting our salt intake?" Though, of course, you should always listen to your doctor when it comes to how much salt you can have, if you don't have any medical problems you will probably never get too much salt from home-cooked meals. The salt culprits are things like canned soups, frozen dinners, and deli meats. So if you're making a nutritious *Meat on the Side* meal from scratch, there should be no concern over the amount of salt you are adding as you are starting with ingredients that are, for the most part, natu-rally low in sodium.

PS. All of my recipes call for unsalted butter; if you use salted you will want to use less salt.

PPS. Chefs like to use the word "seasoned" instead of "salted," so next time you think a dish needs more salt say it's "underseasoned" and you'll sound like the chef that you are.

PPPS. Who knew I could write so much about salt?! Moving on . . .

Black pepper. I like pepper, but I don't love it like some people. To me it has a very strong taste, so instead of automatically adding it to my recipes I like to take a step back and think if I really want that flavor in the dish. Because of this you won't see as much pepper in this book as with other cookbooks, but if you live by the motto "where there is salt, there is pepper!" then go ahead and add it, or add more than I've specified.

Chiles (hot peppers). I love using fresh chiles in recipes. It's always great to have some crushed red pepper flakes on hand, but a fresh chile gives you heat along with big flavor, which the dried flakes don't really have. Look for fresh jalapeños, cherry peppers, Thai chiles, or serranos in your grocery store. I suggest always removing the seeds and ribs of the chile to keep the heat in check. The only problem with fresh chiles is that one jalapeño can be much hotter than the next, so sometimes I cook hot peppers on the side and add as much as I like to the final dish. Or if you're brave, bite right into a little of the raw pepper to get an idea of its spice level. Or make your husband do it.

Fresh versus dried herbs. I LOVE fresh herbs, I think they make all the difference, but if you don't use them enough, consider growing them on your windowsill so they are there when-ever you need. When using dried herbs instead of fresh the general rule of thumb is to use a third of the amount, so if the recipe calls for 1 tablespoon fresh oregano you will want to use 1 teaspoon dried. However sometimes fresh herbs are hard to replace with dried, for instance fresh cilantro has a very different flavor from dried. So when it comes to a delicate herb like cilantro or basil, if you can't find it fresh, it's better to sub something like fresh parsley instead of using the dried version. At the end of the day this is not an exact formula, so taste as you go and adjust.

Acknowledgments

TO MY HUSBAND, EVAN, YOU ARE MUCH MORE than my rock; you are my favorite person; you are my inspiration, my love, my everything. Without your never-ending love and support I wouldn't be where I am and I would not be who I am. You have always believed in me and never thought my dreams were crazy (even when they were). I will never find the appropriate words to thank you for all you do for me. I love you so very much.

To Anthony Mattero at Foundry Literary + Media, you were the first one to believe in this book and believe in me as an author. It's amazing to see what has grown from that one e-mail! I appreciate you for your enthusiasm and knowledge and for your endless guidance with this first-time author. I am very lucky to have you beside me on this journey.

To BJ Berti at St. Martin's Press, from moment one I knew you were the person to help me bring this book to life. You have given me the perfect amount of both direction and creative license. And your expertise and attention to detail are why this book is so great. I thank you for believing in me and seeing the potential in my idea.

To Courtney, thank you for all your hard work and for always giving me your positive energy even through e-mails.

To Michelle, Shubhani, and James, somehow you were able to know what I wanted and what this book needed before I did. Your work is beautiful, flawless, and enhances the recipes and words throughout these pages. And a huge thank-you

to the rest of the team at St. Martin's Press; your enthusiasm and hard work do not go unnoticed.

To Carol Spier, you are simply irreplaceable. Thank you for taking the manuscript from good to great. You have given this book so much of your creative energy and time and it shows through every page. You have listened to every idea of mine (even the bad ones) and helped me to make the best decisions. You have corrected my grammar mistakes (over and over and over again) while never losing my voice. You're simply the best.

To Ellen Silverman, thank you for caring about this project as much as I do. And thank you for making my vision a reality. Your gorgeous photographs have literally made the book I dreamed up in my head come to life. And for that I will forever be in your debt.

To Bette Blau, I didn't know how much I needed you until I had you, and now I'm not letting go. Thank you for making this book a true representation of myself (with a Bette touch). Your style and spirit can be seen through these pages.

To Roscoe Betsill, your tireless work preparing the recipes and dedication to representing my food at its best has resulted in mouthwatering pictures that people will never be able to resist. Thank you for your food and your humor.

To Mike and Liz, you both have been such amazing friends to Evan and me. You allowed me to claim your incredible house as my own, and I can never truly pay you back. Thank you for your generosity, and most important thank you for your support and friendship. I am so very lucky to have you both in my life.

To Bodhitree Farm, this cover would not be as beautiful without your amazing veggies. And thank you to Bedford Cheese Shop and Migliorelli Farm for providing us the perfect backdrop to many of these photos.

To Blue Water Grill and Chris, if I'm not cooking I want to be eating your food. Thank you for allowing us to take over your beautiful restaurant and for being the perfect host. And a big thank-you to Amber, for not only making this happen but for being an amazing support system, assistant, and friend.

To my family, you bring the joy to my life and have always helped me keep the fire inside me burning. I couldn't do it without you and I would never want to. I love you all so much more than you could possibly imagine and I'm happy to be your permanent chef on holidays, birthdays, and any other time you'll have me. Love you guys.

To Gina, Frankie, Alexis, and Kelly, nothing make me happier than seeing your smiling faces throughout this book. I appreciate you all for taking the time to shoot these photos and I love that the world can see what amazing and beautiful friends and family I have.

To my followers and fans, your enthusiasm for *Meat on the Side* is what has made this dream come true. Thank you for your endless support and good wishes. I'll never be able to truly express how grateful I am for each and every one of you.

Index